ATH ATH.............Hello? Hello? ....   CONNECTING   Please enter password

E

MAIL
ADDRESSES
OF THE
RICH
&
FAMOUS

BY SETH GODIN

ADDISON-WESLEY PUBLISHING COMPANY

Reading, Massachusetts • Menlo Park, California • New York
Don Mills, Ontario • Wokingham, England • Amsterdam
Bonn • Sydney • Singapore • Tokyo • Madrid • San Juan
Paris • Seoul • Milan • Mexico City • Taipei

Library of Congress Cataloging-in-Publication Data

Godin, Seth.
    E-Mail addresses of the rich & famous / Seth Godin.
       p. cm.
    Includes index.
    ISBN 0-201-40893-7
       1. Celebrities--Directories. 2. Electronic mail systems-
    -Directories. I. Title II. Title: E-Mail addresses of the rich
    and famous.
CT120.G65 1994
920.009'04--dc20   94-10438
                                                          CIP

Sponsoring Editor: David Clark...djclark@holonet.net
Project Manager: Joanne Clapp Fullagar...x0177@applelink.apple.com
Production Coordinator: Gail McDonald Jordan...aw.prod@applelink.apple.com
Head Researcher: Jonathan Hurwitz...jon@sgp.com
Text design: Karen Engelman...karen@sgp.com
Cover design: Jean Seal...seal.j@applelink.apple.com.

3 4 5 6 7 8-DOH-9897969594
Third printing, September 1994

Addison-Wesley books are available for bulk purchases by corporations, institutions, and other organizations. For more information please contact the Corporate, Government and Special Sales Department at (800) 238-9682.

Dedicated to the spirit of the Internet and to the people who maintain that spirit. To Jane Metcalfe, Louis Rossetto, Chris Locke, Steve Case, Mary Kay Fenner, Alex Nikifortchuk, Jim McBride, Vinton Cerf, Bob LeVitus, Guy Kawasaki, Peter H. Lewis, and the thousands of anonymous net surfers who make cyberspace a neighborhood.

And to Alexander Godin and Olivia Clark, cyberspace navigators of the next century.

CONTENTS

#: 122909 S2/Star Trek 10-Apr-87 00:48:21 Sb: #122798-STTNG News Fm:

INTRODUCTION

I love e-mail. Every time the little "You've got mail" announcement sounds, my heart beats a little quicker. What unknown treasure, unexpected kudos or undeserved flame lies in my mailbox?

E-mail is more than just fast mail. It is an entirely new form of communication. It seems like "considered communication" to me. You get the speed of a phone call with the reflection of a letter. No one would ever send a one-line letter by Federal Express, but short e-mail responses are the norm. It's hard to imagine letting 2,000 people in on your correspondence with someone, but it happens with e-mail all the time.

This book was designed to do what no other has ever attempted—to increase communication between the movers & shakers and the rest of us. Believe it or not, most "celebrities" are not inundated with fan e-mail. They don't entirely "vant to be alone"—they wouldn't be online if they weren't as curious about what's going on out there as we are. Similarly, many businesses, editors, writers, and researchers are online because they would like more contact with the outside world, not less.

Careful! The door to the world of uncensored e-mail is held open quite precariously. With automated mail readers and screening software, influential power brokers could easily cut off communication with the rest of us. Bill Gates was receiving eight letters a week from unknown outsiders—until a *New Yorker* article upped his mail load to 5,000. Ouch. Do everyone a favor and don't bother sending mail to someone who wouldn't appreciate reading the message you've sent. Thoughtful letters on relevant topics will generate far more interesting discourse.

A NEW CONVENTION

A simple new convention will allow easy communication without overloading the system. When you send a message to someone, you need to include a subject. Just follow these two rules when mailing to someone you don't know:

If you're sending unsolicited mail, precede your subject with a ?.

If you're sending a commercially related piece of mail, precede your subject with a $.

This is a courtesy that will allow people to screen their mail and increases the chances that your mail will be read by someone who *wants* to read it.

I love getting mail, and so far I've managed to find the time to respond to everyone who writes to me. If you've got comments or suggestions on this book, please drop me a line: SGP@SGP.COM. If you'd like to get a free copy of the second edition of this book, just send along some names we left out. If we include at least two of the names you send, we'll send you a complimentary copy.

A NOTE ABOUT THE ADDRESSES

For consistency, we've listed all addresses in standard Internet format. You can use this to send mail from all leading commercial services, as well as from an Internet connection. Of course, if you are sending mail to someone who happens to be on the same service as you are, you should truncate the address. For example: 1234.234@compuserve.com becomes 1234,234 for intra-compuserve mail. In the case of addresses ending with @aol.com, just strip that suffix if you are already on AOL. Check with your provider for details

Note that CompuServe is currently charging a fifteen-cent fee for all incoming Internet mail. Please send mail to CompuServe users with restraint, and be sure that your subject line clearly states what your message is about.

Here is a list of the suffixes used by each major online service. To convert an address to Internet format, you can usually follow these steps:
- Delete spaces
- Convert commas to periods
- Add the appropriate suffix

AMERICA ONLINE	@aol.com

The suffix for America Online users

APPLELINK	@applelink.apple.com

The suffix for Applelink users

ATTMAIL	@attmail.com

The suffix for AT&T mail users

BIX	@dcibix.das.net

The suffix for Bix users

COMPUSERVE	@compuserve.com

The suffix for Compuserve users

DELPHI	@delphi.com

The suffix for Delphi users

EASYNET	@host.enet.dec.com

The suffix for EasyNet users

MCIMAIL	@mcimail.com

The suffix for MCI Mail users

PEACENET	@igc.org

The suffix for Peacenet users

ACKNOWLEDGMENTS

My e-mail career started in 1976, at Williamsville South High School. Thanks to Mrs. Eaton who let me play. Also thanks to Linda Litner, Guy Kawasaki, Dan Lovy, Dan Levy, Ellen Miles, Jon Schull, Vic Lapuszynski, Martin Erb, and Bob Jacoby, e-mail pen pals all.

This book wouldn't exist without Jonathan Hurwitz, a hot-shot Internet guru we were lucky enough to snag. Thanks to Alex Nikifortchuk, Steve Case, Robert Gehorsam, Liz Levin and Mary Kay Fenner, who have supported our work in many ways.

This book came to be because the swirling winds of creativity caused several great ideas to come together in one place. Thanks to David Clark at Addison-Wesley for crystallizing it and finding me to create the book.

We received input and addresses from hundreds of online gurus, too many to list here. Ultimately, though, the information in this book is our responsibility, so feel free to drop us a line with your feedback.

ABOUT THE AUTHOR

Seth Godin has written (under his own name or using a pseudonym) more than 400 books, including *Valley of the Dolls, The Eiger Sanction, Catcher in the Rye, The Cat in the Hat* and many others.

In addition to his ghostwriting talents, Godin has created more than forty books on a variety of topics, ranging from *Zero Gravity Gardening Techniques* to *How to Build a Brick Pizza Oven That Will Even Melt Cheese.*

His hobbies include piloting nuclear submarines, snail ranching and raising those adorable little Sea Monkeys® that you see on the back of comic books.

NOTE: The dialogue in the sidebars comes from *Are Tribbles Kosher?* a CompuServe file that recounts a conversation between David Gerrold, the writer of the famous "Trouble With Tribbles" Star Trek episode and numerous fans.

will make that decision? Gadzooks! Is this the <*shudder*> End Of The Tribbles?

A DAY IN THE LIFE OF AN ON-LINE ADDICT

by Bob "Dr. Macintosh" LeVitus

My name is Bob LeVitus and I'm an on-line addict. Fortunately, this is the only addiction I know of that is actually good for you, which is a darn good thing, considering how much time I spend connected by modem to something or another (see below).

As a writer, my modem is as essential to me as my telephone or fax machine. I work with my editors almost exclusively through e-mail; my proposals, finished articles, and book chapters—all complete with illustrations—travel back and forth through the ether on a daily basis (thank heaven for StuffIt). I do research online that used to require time-consuming trips to the library. And best of all, I'm able to carry on dozens of virtual conversations at once with people who are actually using the software and hardware I write about. Simply put, I love being connected. My modem makes it possible for me to do more work in less time and do better work with less effort. Online communication has changed my life for the better, in so many ways. Don't be surprised if it changes yours.

See you on line.

A typical day at Rancho del LeVitus:

5:45 a.m. The Mac turns on, then automatically launches CompuServe Navigator and runs a session script that logs on, gets my e-mail, scans all the messages in 20 or 25 forums, including the ZiffNet MacUser forums and several MAUG forums, then logs off. (Technology for this feat is provided by Sophisticated Circuits PowerKey and CE Software's QuicKeys.)

6:00 a.m. Accompanied by a very large cup of french roast, I review the Navigator session, replying to e-mail and forum messages as appropriate.

6:20 a.m. I run the Navigator script that sends all the replies I just wrote.

6:25 a.m. I log on to America Online, read and reply to my e-mail, then check out the action in a few forums—usually the Macintosh Business, Games, and Utilities forums, at the very least.

6:45 a.m. I log onto AppleLink to check and reply to my e-mail there. I try hard not to spend much time—AppleLink is soooo expensive.

8:00 to noon This is my time for writing and/or evaluating new software and hardware. Still, chances are good that I've logged onto CompuServe at least once, more than likely to find something in Computer Database or Magazine Database, a pair of full-text databases that allow you to search through millions of magazine articles.

1:00 to 4:00 p.m. More writing and/or evaluating products.

4:00 p.m. I run my Navigator e-mail and forum script again.

4:20 p.m. I review the Navigator session, replying to e-mail and forum messages as appropriate.

4:40 p.m. I run the Navigator script that sends all the replies I just wrote.

4:50 p.m. I log onto America Online again, to check my e-mail.

Footnotes: If I go back in the office after dinner (my office is in my home), as I often do, chances are I'll log onto both CompuServe and America Online at least one more time each, just to see if I've received any new mail. A couple of times a week I also log onto my excellent user group BBS, CapMac Online, to check my e-mail and read a few folders worth of messages. I try to check my e-mail on GEnie, MCI Mail, and Delphi at least once a week.

Bob "Dr. Macintosh" LeVitus has been a contributing editor for MacUser for many years and is the author of twelve computer books including Dr. Macintosh's Guide to the On-Line Universe *from Addison-Wesley, and* Guide to the Macintosh Underground *from Hayden Books.*

E-MAIL IS THE CURSE OF THE LURKING CLASS!

Vinton G. Cerf
President, Internet Society
Senior Vice President, MCI Data Services

If ever I needed an anecdote about the impact of e-mail on my life and career, the request from the editors of this book to write these brief remarks offers as good an example as any.

It is 2:43 a.m. here in Camelot (Annandale, Virginia) as I type these words. What am I doing up at this hour? I am trying to clear my inbox of some 400 messages that accumulated over a period of three short days while I was off doing something else. E-mail is a lot like a major output of a cattle feed lot — if you don't get rid of it quick, you will be buried in it. I haven't tried using e-mail to fertilize my roses, however... hmm.

I have been using e-mail literally since it was introduced to the ARPANET community in the early 1970s. It has had a very significant impact on my career.

For one thing, it turns out I am severely hearing impaired (about 55-60 dB loss in each ear). While this is largely corrected by hearing aids, colleagues will tell you I can still manage to miss a lot. If I had had to conduct a career in network research and development relying on telephones and face-to-face meetings alone, I think it would have been difficult to impossible. E-mail evened the floor, so to speak, and had the other salient feature of dealing with time zone differences.

Speaking of the latter, it seems to have required me to sleep not at all—thereby solving the time zone problem :-).

In point of fact, e-mail is really quite a distinct medium from other forms of interpersonal communication. One of the most interesting aspects is that, because it is computer-manipulable, it can serve as well as a path of communication between programs and between people and programs. One can imagine sending mail to a program to get something done, just as one might send mail to a person for the same purpose.

Of course, we are still some distance away from reasonably intelligent programs that can accept as input casual natural language and take action on it—but the general idea of interacting with intelligent agents as if they were, well, at least trainable, seems very appealing.

Over time, e-mail has evolved to include the ability to carry a variety of objects as part of the message: voice, multi-font text, digital images, video clips, programs, and so on. The common thread of digital representations is a unifying factor in the otherwise very heterogeneous world of computer-based information. Over time, it is to be hoped that object representation standards will emerge to bring more interoperability to the e-mail-enabled applications emerging from the creative cauldron of Internet exploration. Perhaps one will be able to say with some veracity, "See you on the Net!" and the meaning may well be taken literally as well as figuratively. One hopes so.

See you on the Net!

THE
ADDRESSES

ACADEMICS

CHRIS ADAMEC   71216.105@compuserve.com
Adoption Advocate

BONNIE BLAGOJEVIC   bonnieb@maine.maine.edu
Department of Education expert

DALE DEBOER   drdeboer.uccs.edu
Economist

CHERYL GARNETT   cgarnett@esusda.gov
Education

JIM HARTLEY   jehartley@ucdavis.edu
Noted economist and spelling expert

LIBBY HUBBARD   neutopia@educ.umass.edu
Radical educator, futurist

PAUL JOSEPH   72072.146@compuserve.com
Law professor, Nova University

DAVID KRISTOFFERSON   kristoff@net.bio.net
Moderator, International Newsgroups for Molecular Biology

JOSE MESEGUER	meseguer@csl.sri.com

Algebraic specifications expert

JAMES MITCHELL	jmitchel@inet.ed.gov

Education

JACK PELTASON	jack.peltason@ucop.edu

President, University of California

GLENN REYNOLDS	71340.1313@compuserve.com

Law Professor, University of Tennessee

RON RIVEST	rivest@mit.edu

Mathematician; developer of RSA cryptography system

MICHAEL ROTHSCHILD	bionomix@well.sf.ca.us

Organizational learning economist

MOSHE SIPPER	moshes@math.tau.ac.il

Computer scientist

PAUL SOUTHWORTH	pauls@umich.edu

Political archivist

IAN TAYLOR	I.Taylor@sociology.salford.ac.uk

Criminology revisionist

ARTIFICIAL INTELLIGENCE EXPERTS

HAL ABELSON   hal@martigny.ai.mit.edu
Artificial intelligence researcher

JOHN MCCARTHY   jmc@sail.stanford.edu
Artificial intelligence theorist

MARVIN MINSKY   minsky@ai.mit.edu
Father of artificial intelligence, director, MIT Media Lab

CHRISTIAN QUEINNEC   queinnec@margaux.inria.fr
Lisp expert

AUTHORS

DOUGLAS ADAMS   76206.2507@compuserve.com
Author of The Hitchhiker's Guide to the Galaxy

SCOTT ADAMS   scottadams@aol.com
Cartoonist, Dilbert

PHIL AGRE   pagre@ucsd.edu
Author of Computation and Human Experience

DAVID ANGELL   dangell@shell.portal.com
Author of The Instant Internet Guide

ROBERT ASPIRIN   76254.523@compuserve.com
Science fiction writer

DOUGLAS BELL   dougbell@netcom.com
Author of Van Gogh in Space

NATHANIEL BRANDEN   73117.607@compuserve.com
Writer, associate of Ayn Rand

RICK BROADHEAD   ysar1111@vm1.yorku.ca
Co-author of Canadian Internet Handbook

JUDITH BROADHURST   70421.2063@compuserve.com
Writer

CHRIS BUNCH   73354.3157@compuserve.com
Science fiction writer

ORSON SCOTT CARD   70044.3107@compuserve.com
Science fiction writer

TOM CARGILL   cargill@fruug.org
Author of C++ Programming Style

JIM CARROLL   jcarroll@jacc.com
Co-author of Canadian Internet Handbook

TOM CLANCY   tomclancy@aol.com
Author of The Hunt for Red October *and other techno-thrillers*

ALLAN COLE   75130.2761@compuserve.com
Science fiction writer

RICHARD E. CYTOWIC   p00907@psilink.com
Expert on synesthesia; author of The Man Who Tasted Shapes

FREDERIC E. DAVIS   3057504@mci-mail.com
Author of The Windows Bible

JOHN DECEMBER   decemj@rpi.edu
Author of The Internet and Computer-Mediated Communication

MICHAEL DRINKARD   miked@phantom.com
Author of Disobedience

GEORGE EFFINGER   76050.1300@compuserve.com
Science fiction writer

RAYMOND E. FEIST	76657.2776@compuserve.com

Science fiction writer

DAVID FELDMAN	feldman@pipeline.com

Author of the Imponderables *books*

JOE FLOWER	bbear@well.sf.ca.us

Author of Prince of the Magic Kingdom: Michael Eisner and the Making of Disney

ROBERT FULGHUM	70771.763@compuserve.com

Author of Everything I Ever Needed to Know I Learned in Kindergarten

JIM GASPERINI	jimg@well.sf.ca.us

Author of Hidden Agenda

DAVID GERROLD	70307.544@compuserve.com

Underrated science fiction writer, inventor of the Tribble

JAMES GLEICK	gleick@pipeline.com

Biographer of Richard P. Feynman

JOHN E. GRISHAM	71035.1742@compuserve.com

Author of The Pelican Brief, The Firm

BRENT HESLOP	bheslop@shell.portal.com

Author of The Instant Internet Guide

DOUGLAS HOFSTADTER	dughof@cogsci.indiana.edu

Author of Goedel, Escher, Bach

GUY KAWASAKI	76703.3031@compuserve.com

Mac guru

BRENDAN KEHOE   brendan@cygnus.com

Author of Zen and the Art of the Internet; *author of Archie*

FLOYD KEMSKE   73437.50@compuserve.com

Writer

ED KROL   e-krol@uiuc.edu

Author of The Whole Internet, *the breakthrough book on the net*

MIKE KUBE-MCDOWELL   73740.15@compuserve.com

Author of Exile, Quiet Pool

JOSEPH J. LAZZARO   lazzaro@world.std.com

Author of Adaptive Computer Technology for the Disabled

EVELYN C. LEEPER   ecl@cbnews.cb.att.com

Book reviewer

BOB LEVITUS   76004.2076@compuserve.com

Author of Dr. Macintosh's Guide to the Online Universe

MIKE LEVY   73374.1473@compuserve.com

President, Outdoor Writers Association of America

TOM MADDOX   Tmaddox@halcyon.com

Writer

ANNE MCCAFFREY   72007.45@compuserve.com

Science fiction writer

VONDA N. MCINTYRE   72077.61@compuserve.com

Science fiction writer

PAT MCMANUS   72010.511@compuserve.com

Humorist

JUDITH MCNAUGHT   76416.1065@compuserve.com
Romance novelist

TONI MORRISON   morrison@pucc.princeton.edu
Novelist, Nobel Prize-winner

JOHN PARK   af250@freenet.carleton.ca
Writer

DANA RAE POMEROY   73150.1164@compuserve.com
Author of When Someone You Love Has Cancer

TERRY PRATCHETT   tpratchett@unseen.demon.co.uk
Science fiction writer

JOHN QUARTERMAN   jsa@tic.com
Author of The Matrix (Internet and Services Guide)

ERIC RAYMOND   esr@snark.thrysus.com
Editor, New Hacker's Dictionary

GLENN REID   glenn@rightbrain.com
Author of PostScript Language Program Design

MIKE RESNICK   76266.1641@compuserve.com
Science fiction writer

RUDY RUCKER   rucker@sjsumcs.sjsuedu
Science fiction writer, mathematician

SORELLE SAIDMAN   72674.3644@compuserve.com
Author of Bryan Adams: Everything He Does

DAVID SANDERSON   dws@ora.com
Author of the second book written about smileys

DAVID SANDERSON   dws@ora.com
Author of the second book written about smileys

JACK SARFATTI   sarfatti@netcom.com
Writer

ROBERT J. SAWYER   76702.747@compuserve.com
Science fiction writer

MIKE SHANNON   datamike@interaccess.com
Writer, Underground Mac Report

HARRY SPENCER   henry@zoo.toronto.edu
Sci.space authority

ROBERT STACK   70243.3205@compuserve.com
Writer

BRUCE STERLING   bruces@phantom.com
Author of Hacker Crackdown

LINDA STERN   72160.1546@compuserve.com
Writer

W. RICHARD STEVENS   netbook@hsi.com
Author of Unix Network Programming

CLIFF STOLL   cliff@cfa.harvard.edu
Author of The Cuckoo's Egg, *about the search for a hacker*

NANCY TAMOSUITIS   nancyt@phantom.com
Author of The Joy of CyberSex

CHARLES TART   cttart@ucdavis.edu
Author of Altered States of Consciousness

74276,662 To: Ilene Schneider 72467,3255 (X) I think they're a form of

TODD TIBBETS   ttl@netcom.com

Editor, The Unplastic News

ANDREW TOBIAS   70641.473@compuserve.com

Investor, noted writer

HAL VARIAN   hal.varian@umich.edu

Noted economist and writer

VERNOR VINGE   vrv@cimage.com

Author of True Names...and Other Dangers

VIC WINKLER   winkler_vic@gistd_mail.prc.com

Authority on network security

JOSEPH ZITT   jzitt@bga.com

Poet, performer

CELEBRITIES

EDWARD ASNER   72726.357@compuserve.com
Actor

John Perry Barlow   barlow@eff.org
Songwriter for the Grateful Dead

DON BARRETT   72253.2172@compuserve.com
Writer, director, producer of Patrick Stewart's The Planets

DAVE BARRY   73314.722@compuserve.com
Humorist, columnist

BEAVIS   beavis@mtv.com
Abrasive cartoon character; Butthead's pal

ALEX BENNETT   abennett@netcom.com
KITS Radio, San Francisco

JAMES BERARDINELLI   blake7@cc.bellcore.com
Movie reviewer

BEST BRAINS, INC.   bbrains@mr.net
Producers, Mystery Science Theater 3000

JORDAN BRADY   73112.731@compuserve.com
MTV show host

TOM BROKAW   nightly@nbc.com
NBC News anchor

JAMES L. BROOKS   72700.2062@compuserve.com
Actor

PAT BUCHANAN   76326.126@compuserve.com
Failed presidential candidate

BUTTHEAD   butthead@mtv.com
Smarter half of Beavis & Butthead

ROBERT CAMPANELL   robcamp@seas.gwu.edu
Producer, Cyberia *television show*

ROGER CARROLL   72212.1002@compuserve.com
Announcer for The Smothers Brothers

JIM CHENEVEY   71021.173@compuserve.com
CBS Radio News

GREGORY COHEN   gcohen@panix.com
New York theater lighting designer

WAYNE COTTER   73223.1667@compuserve.com
Comedian, TV host

DAVID COX   paradox@peg.apc.org
Animator

JOE CRUMMEY   71075.3111@compuserve.com
DJ for KFI, Los Angeles

ADAM CURRY   acurry@mtv.com, adam@mtv.com
MTV VJ

AKI DAMME   adame@snm.com
PBA professional bowler

PETER A. DAVID   pad@cup.portal.com
Marvel Comics writer; Incredible Hulk, X-Men, X-Force

JOHNNY DONOVAN   72567.2022@compuserve.com
DJ for WABC radio, New York

ROGER EBERT   73136.3232@compuserve.com
Movie critic

ALISTAIR FERGUSON   utopia@peg.apc.org
Documentary filmmaker

RICK FISK   risk@auspex.com
Singer, guitarist Rash Behavior

TOD FOLEY   asif@well.sf.ca.us
Writer, producer

ANDREW GARTON   agarton@peg.apc.org
Actor

ROBYN GRIGGS   rgriggs@panix.com
Actress, Another World

CHARLES GRODIN   CharlesGrodin@aol.com
Actor

EVAN HADINGHAM   evan_hadingham@wgbh.org
Science Editor, Nova

ED HALL	76117.1245@compuserve.com

Jay Leno's announcer

JEREMY HALPERN	verge@delphi.com

Actor

PAUL HARRIS	73030.2227@compuserve.com

Radio personality, DC101, Washington, DC

STEVEN HAWORTH	sjh@idm.com

Chicago Theater lighting designer

BOB HOSKINS	75300.1313@compuserve.com

Actor; star of Who Framed Roger Rabbit?

CIARA HUNTER	73404.3631@compuserve.com

Model

BILLY IDOL	idol@well.sf.ca.us, idol@phantom.com

Musician, cyberpunk person

PENN JILLETTE	penn@delphi.com

Comedian and magician; half of Penn & Teller

MIKE JITTLOV	jittlov@gumby.cs.caltech.edu

Filmmaker; producer, director, Ghost, The Wizard of Speed and Time

GARRISON KEILLOR	gkeillor@madmax.mpr.org

National Public Radio personality

WAYNE KNIGHT	71054.2032@compuserve.com

Actor, Seinfeld, Jurassic Park

KURT LARSON	vector@phantom.com

Musician, Information Society

it's tough to feel tender towards a fish. Ever try to pet one or take one out for a.

TOM LEYKIS   73040.2465@compuserve.com
DJ for WRKO, Boston

RUSH LIMBAUGH   70277.2502@compuserve.com
Right-wing political commentator

CARL MALAMUD   info@radio.com
Host, Geek of the Week

MARG MEIKLE   marg_meikle@mindlink.bc.ca
Canadian Broadcasting Corporation (CBC) radio personality

ROBERT W. MORGAN   72427.723@compuserve.com
DJ for KRTH, Los Angeles

JEAN CHRETIEN   primemin@chicken.planet.org
Prime minister of Canada

KEVIN W. MURPHY   71023.3506@compuserve.com
Cast member, Mystery Science Theater 3000

DAVID NERLICH   babel@peg.apc.org
Composer

BRYAN NORCROSS   psmw29a@aol.com
Miami weatherman, hero of Hurricane Hugo

JON NORRIS   jon.norris@aquila.com
Pinball designer at Premier

MILES O'BRIEN   70273.2064@compuserve.com
Science and technology correspondent, CNN

RICHARD ORKIN   74250.110@compuserve.com
Creative radio commercial genius at Orkin Radio Ranch, Los Angeles

RICK OVERTON   72162.1701@compuserve.com

Actor, featured in Groundhog Day, Mrs. Doubtfire

ROCH PARISIEN   75010.2074@compuserve.com

Rock-and-roll songwriter

DONNA PENYAK   71250.356@compuserve.com

CBS Radio News

PAULA POUNDSTONE   paula@mojones.com

Comedian, TV host

JAMES RANDI   72740.456@compuserve.com

Magician, psychic debunker; often on Letterman

TOM RITCHFORD   tom@mvision.com

Electronic wind musician

PHIL ALDEN ROBINSON   72310.1555@compuserve.com

Director, Sneakers *and* Field of Dreams

TRINY ROE   ccroe@cc.uq.oz.au

Filmmaker

STEVEN SALBERG   salberg@main.morris.com

*Professional juggler; member of the board of directors of the
International Jugglers Association*

SAM SIMON   ssimon@aol.com

Creator, The Simpsons, The George Carlin Show

MIKE STEPHENS   mike@snm.com

Saxophonist, The MSP Band

RICK STETTA — rstetta@delphi.com
World champion pinball player

HARRY Z. THOMASON — 73363.2653@compuserve.com
Television producer, presidential buddy

PHILIP TOWER — 75020.227@compuserve.com
Radio personality, WOOD-AM

CLIFF VAN METER — armorine@aol.com
Comic-book artist for Valiant

VICTOR VOLKMAN — victor.volkman@hal9k.com
Video producer

WILLIAM WALKER — bill@snm.com
Professional bowler

MIKE WEBB — rvcmpwebb@aol.com
Theater director

BOB WEST — bobwest1@aol.com
The voice of Barney

KATHLEEN WILLIAMSON — bigk@cs.uq.oz.au
Photographer

BRIAN WILSON — 76340.2231@compuserve.com
Radio personality

JAMES WOODS — jameswoods@aol.com
Actor

CELEBRITIES (PROBABLY FAKES)

BUSBY BERKELEY   busbybrkly@aol.com

Dead movie director

JED CLAMPETT   jedclampet@aol.com

Millionaire oil baron

CECIL B. DEMILLE   cecilbdmil@aol.com

Director

HOWARD THE DUCK   howardduck@aol.com

Movie superhero

ART FLEMING   artfleming@aol.com

And the answer is...

JERRY GARCIA   jgarcia@aol.com

Singer, musician

CEOS, ENTREPRENEURS, AND TITANS OF INDUSTRY

PAM ANGELIS
GEnie

DAVID C. BLANKENHORN
President, SNM, Inc.

BRYAN BOAM
Novell Netware wizard

TOM BOOS
R. R. Donnelley

MARK BUFORD
Northern Telecom

NEAL CAMMY 70431.3102@compuserve.com

UOP

CRAIG CLINE 110–3939@mcimail.com

Seybold

CHERYL CURRID currid@radiomail.net

Founder, Currid & Co.

BARRY DILLER 71043.3616@compuserve.com

Thwarted Hollywood hotshot

DONNALYN FREY 70277.2502@compuserve.com

Frey Communications

R. W. FUNKE funke@usc.edu

President, Red Horse Company

NICHOLAS GRAHAM joeboxer@jboxer.com

President, Joe Boxer Underwear, founder of Underwear Cyberspace

STEVE JOBS sjobs@next.com

Had the Macintosh vision; founder, NeXT Computers

MITCH KAPOR mkapor@eff.org

Founder, Lotus; founder, Electronic Frontier Foundation

NAOMI KARTEN 76217.1620@compuserve.com

Karten & Associates

BRUCE KATZ katz@well.sf.ca.us

Owner, The Well

CHRIS KOENIGSBERG c-koenigsberg@uchicago.edu

Founder, TMI Records

STEPHEN LALIBERTÉ   liberty@bix.com
General Videotex

JON LEBKOWSKY   jonl@io.com
President, FringeWare, Inc.

JOHN MASHEY   mash@mips.com
VP, MIPS Computers

ELLIOT MASIE   76703.4375@compuserve.com
Ziff Institute

LISA MATCHETTE   lisamat@microsoft.com
PR for Microsoft

PAUL MERENBLOOM   70743.3524@compuserve.com
Otsuka American Pharmaceuticals

NANCY MINGUS   71601.2360@compuserve.com
President, Mingus Associates, Inc.

PACO XANDER NATHAN   pacoid@well.sf.ca.us
Co-founder, FringeWare, Inc., and the only person in this book whose middle name starts with X

ROB RAISH   raisch@internet.com
The Internet Company

SETH REICHLIN   seth@prenhall.com
Paramount

DIANE RIBBLE   dribble2@aol.com
PR for America Online

CHARLIE RICHMOND   crichmon@acs.ucalgary.ca
President, Richmond Sound Design, Ltd. (Midi equipment)

MARK RUPORT   ruport@ileaf.com
Interleaf

PETER SCHWARTZ   schwartz@well.sf.ca.us
Co-founder of Global Business Network

PATRICIA SEYBOLD   pseybold@mcimail.com
Part of the Seybold dynasty

BARRY SHEIN   bzs@world.std.com
Software Tool & Die

MICHAEL SPINDLER   spindler@applelink.apple.com
CEO, Apple Computer

BRAD TEMPLETON   brad@clarinet.com
Founder, Clarinet

EDWARD VIELMETTI   emv@msen.com
Vice president, MSEN

TED WAITT   twaitt@bix.com
Founder, Gateway Computers

BILL WASHBURN   washburn@cix.org
Executive director, CIX

REBECCA WETZEL   rwetzel@nic.near.net
Nearnet

PHIL WINTERING   pvw@americast.com
American Cybercasting

night's dinner. Its either that or pop down to the deli and pick up a fresh brisket

COMPUTER VISIONARIES

ALAN KAY   kay2@applelink.apple.com

Co-developer, Xerox Star (father of the Apple Macintosh)

NICHOLAS NEGROPONTE   nicholas@media.mit.com

Multimedia visionary, head of the media lab at MIT

JEF RASKIN   raskin@well.sf.ca.us

One of the geniuses behind the Macintosh

DENNIS RITCHIE   dmr@tempel.research.att.com

Creator of C and Unix

MARK STAHLMAN   stahlman@radiomail.net

New Media Association

KEN THOMPSON   ken@research.att.com

Father of C, Unix with Dennis Ritchie, Turing Award winner

RICHARD WURMAN   wurman@medialab.media.mit.edu

Self-hyped wunderkind luminary

CONGRESS, LEGISLATORS AND STAFF

Congress is slowly adopting e-mail. Most of those listed below are minions and acolytes—the actual legislators are identified as such.

DOREEN ALBISTON   dalbisto@hr.house.gov

House of Representatives

RON AUFIERO   raufiero@hr.house.gov

House of Representatives

MIKE BARTELL   mike_bartell@scc.senate.gov

Senate

JACK BELCHER   jbelcher@hr.house.gov

House of Representatives

TED BLAKE   tblake@hr.house.gov

House of Representatives, House Information Systems

GARY BRIDGEWATER   gbridge@charm.isi.edu

White House

BUCK BURGESS   lburgess@hr.house.gov
House of Representatives

CHRIS CASEY   ccasey@hr.house.gov
Senate

CONGRESSIONAL COMMENT DESK   comments@hr.house.gov
General address for feedback to Congress, mail is then distributed

SAM COOPERSMITH   samaz01@hr.house.gov
Member of Congress, Arizona, 1st District

JAY DICKEY   jdickey@hr.house.gov
Member of Congress, Arkansas, 4th District

SENATOR CHRISTOPHER DODD   sendodd@dodd.senate.gov
Senator, Connecticut

SAM GEJDENSON   bozrah@hr.house.gov
Member of Congress, Connecticut, 2nd District

NEWT GINGRICH   georgia6@hr.house.gov
Member of Congress, Georgia, 6th District

MICHAEL HARRIS   ontpc@chicken.planet.org
Leader, Ontario Progressive Conservative Party

BOB HENSHAW   bhenshaw@hr.house.gov
House of Representatives

TED KENNEDY   ccasey@hr.house.gov
Senator, Massachusetts

BOB KERREY   tschoeb@hr.house.gov
Senator, Nebraska

LYN McLEOD   ontlib@chicken.planet.org
Leader, Ontario Liberal Party

GEORGE MILLER   georgem@hr.house.govhr.house.gov
Member of Congress, California, 7th District

CHARLIE ROSE   crose@hr.house.gov
Member of Congress, North Carolina 7th District

TIM SCHOEB   tschoeb@hr.house.gov
Senate

KAREN SHEPHERD   shepherd@hr.house.gov
Member of Congress, Utah 2nd District

MARGARET SHUGRUE   mshugrue@hr.house.gov
Senate

PETE STARK   petemail@hr.house.gov
Member of Congress, California 13th District

MEL WATT   melmail@hr.house.gov
Member of Congress, North Carolina 12th District

KIM WINN   kim_winn@scc.senate.gov
Senate

EDITORS AND PUBLISHERS

MIKE ANBINDER   mha@baka.ithaca.ny.us
News editor, TidBITS

BRETT ANDERSON   76646.3722@compuserve.com
Editor-in-chief, Portable Computing *magazine*

ERIN ASHBY   75570.2561@compuserve.com
The Columbus Journal

TOM AVRO   73330.1335@compuserve.com
Digital Digest

MIKE AZZARA   mikea@ost.com
Editor, Open Systems Today

JOHN BANKS   71234.637@compuserve.com
Sombrero

NIKI BARRIE   74756.445@compuserve.com
Ducks Unlimited

JOHN BARTIMOLE   71041.3310@compuserve.com
Shooting Sports Retailer

RICHARD D. BARTLETT   73374.1107@compuserve.com
Contributing editor, The Reptiles

LISA BEARNSON   76004.3617@compuserve.com
Editor, WordPerfect *magazine*

ALLEN BIEHL   76004.3620@compuserve.com
WordPerfect for Windows

BILL BLINN   74365.1543@compuserve.com
Today's Parts Manager

DEBORAH BRANSCUM   branscum@aol.com
Editor, MacWorld

GARETH BRANWYN   gareth2@aol.com
Senior editor, bOING bOING

JIM BROKER   70717.1343@compuserve.com
Squaw Creek Journal

JOHN BROWNING   browning@well.sf.ca.us
Contributing editor, Wired

MICHAEL BURGARD   mikeb@uworld.com
Contributing editor, UnixWorld

RON BURK   ronb@rdpub.com
Editor, Windows/DOS Developers Journal

JIM BURTON   75300.2316@compuserve.com
PC Home Journal

BRUCE CAMERON   71171.1344@compuserve.com

Law & Order

T. CARROLL   71550.133@compuserve.com

Editor-in-chief, Santa Clara County High Tech Law Journal

BILL CLEDE   76702.2011@compuserve.com

Technical editor, Law and Order *magazine*

CLARE CONLEY   76057.3613@compuserve.com

Former editor-in-chief, Outdoor Life *magazine*

CSABA CSERE   71234.273@compuserve.com

Editor-in-Chief, Car & Driver *magazine*

RIP CUNNINGHAM   76424.1525@compuserve.com

Salt Water Sportsman

FREDDIE DAWKINS   70624.557@compuserve.com

EEMA Briefing

DANIEL DERN   ddern@world.std.com

Editor, Internet World

DAVID DIAMOND   davidd@uworld.com

Managing editor, UnixWorld

EDITOR   2600@well.sf.ca.us

2600 Hacker's Quarterly

EDITOR   74160.162@compuserve.com

Air Quality Week

EDITOR   70370.702@compuserve.com

MacWorld

EDITOR   fortyhex@phantom.com

FortyHex, The Virus Writers' Journal

EDITOR   axcess@aol.com

aXcess *magazine*

EDITOR   editor@chronicle.merit.edu

Chronicle of Higher Education

EDITOR   compute@aol.com

COMPUTE *magazine*

EDITOR   cgw@aol.com

Computer Gaming World

EDITOR   gsmag@aol.com

GS+ *magazine*

EDITOR   homeoffice@aol.com

Home Office Computing

EDITOR   incider@aol.com

*in*Cider

EDITOR   markvoor@phantom.com

Information Law Alert

EDITOR   iym@aol.com

IYM Software Review

EDITOR   mondo2k@phantom.com

Mondo 2000 Online

EDITOR   edit@newmedia.com

New Media

EDITOR   nibble@aol.com

Nibble *magazine*

EDITOR   76247.1270@compuserve.com

NSSF News & Views

EDITOR   pcnovice@aol.com

PC Today

EDITOR   71517.2176@compuserve.com

Shooter's Rag

ADAM ENGST   72511.306@compuserve.com

Editor, TidBITS

DAVE ERNST   74230.167@compuserve.com

Farmers Digest

BRIAN ERWIN   brian@ora.com

O'Reilly & Associates

GARRY FAIRBAIRN   76475.606@compuserve.com

The Western Producer

RIK FARROW   rik@uworld.com

Technical editor, UnixWorld

JON FEUERHELM   jonf@uworld.com

Assistant managing editor, UnixWorld

SUSAN CANBY FIFER   netgo3@capcon.net

National Geographic

DAVE FLACK   davef@uworld.com

Editor-in-chief, UnixWorld

PAUL GILLIN   76537.2413@compuserve.com
Computerworld

SETH GODIN   sgp@sgp.com
Seth Godin Productions

CHRIS GOGGANS   erikb@phantom.com
Editor, Phrack *magazine*

JOSHUA GREENBAUM   jgreenbaum@mcimail.com
European correspondent, UnixWorld

STEVE GREENHOW   73557.1143@compuserve.com
True Imaging

JAY GROSS   72517.326@compuserve.com
Southeastern Wildlife and Waterfowl

PATRICK GROTE   71031.335@compuserve.com
The PC Journal

BRENT GROVES   71760.660@compuserve.com
American Conservative Monthly

MARILYN HALDANE   71543.1541@compuserve.com
Hand in Hand

TOM HARGADON   foxhedge@well.sf.ca.us
Publisher, The Green Sheet

DAVID HARRIS   73057.2663@compuserve.com
Canadian Alpine Journal

ELLEN KEY HARRIS   ekh@panix.com
Editor, Ballantine Del Rey

by halacha, or haggadah? To go to the heart of the matter... If the hoof is divided

PATRICK NEILSEN HAYDEN   pnh@panix.com

Senior editor, Tor Books

KEN HIRES   71303.613@compuserve.com

Western Wilderness

ROB HOARE   72461.3361@compuserve.com

Baldrine Publishing

MARTIN HOFFMAN   100144.447@compuserve.com

Outdoor *magazine*

ANDREW HUTCHISON   100236.3005@compuserve.com

Off Campus

WALTER JEFFRIES   73130.1734@compuserve.com

Flash

DON JOHNSON   71631.42@compuserve.com

Executive Editor, PC Presentations and Productions

RICHARD KADREY   kadrey@well.sf.ca.us

Senior editor, FutureSex *magazine; science fiction novelist*

BRUCE KAUFFMAN   72520.1674@compuserve.com

HealthQuest

KAY KEPPLER   72212.3256@compuserve.com

Senior Editor, AI Expert

JAY KINNEY   jay@well.sf.ca.us

Publisher of Gnosis: A Journal of Western Inner Traditions

JAKE KIRCHNER   5668331@mcimail.com

Executive editor, Windows Buyer's Guide

KERRY KNUDSEN   70703.300@compuserve.com

Michigan Outdoor Journal

FRED LANGA   5698334@mcimail.com

Editorial director, Windows Buyer's Guide

DAN LAVIN   @networld.com

Senior editor, Nextworld

JAYNE LEVIN   helen@access.digex.com

Publisher, The Internet Letter

STEVE LEWERS   lewers@hmco.com

Vice president, Houghton Mifflin

ALBERT LEWIS   70544.3642@compuserve.com

Art in Architecture

LES LINE   76702.2102@compuserve.com

Former editor, Audubon *magazine*

JEFF LUCIA   72360.1250@compuserve.com

Rescue *magazine*

BILL MACHRONE   72241.15@compuserve.com

PC *Magazine*

ERIC MAFFEI   ericm@microsoft.com

Editor-in-chief, Microsoft Systems Journal

GEORGE MARGELIS   76304.3672@compuserve.com

Alternative Computing

JOHN E. MARTIN   70304.2276@compuserve.com

TI*BIZ

SIMON MCCAFFERY   76216.3013@compuserve.com
BASSIN' *and* Crappie *magazine*

BONNIE MCGHEE   bonniem@uworld.com
Editorial administration, UnixWorld

JANE METCALFE   jane@wired.com
President, Wired *magazine*

ART MICHAELS   76247.624@compuserve.com
Boat Pennsylvania *and* Pennsylvania Angler

STEVEN MIKES   editor@unx.com
Editor-in-chief, The X Journal

JUDITH MILHOUN   stjude@phantom.com
Former editor, Mondo 2000

DON NORRIS   100032.1151@compuserve.com
Horwitz Grahame Publications

HENRY NUWER   76004.1761@compuserve.com
Arts Indiana *magazine*

LARRY O'BRIEN   76702.705@compuserve.com
Editor-in-chief, AI Expert

JIM OLDHAM   76507.1702@compuserve.com
The Fisherman Florida

RYAN PAIGE   71172.3532@compuserve.com
Campus *magazine*

JEROD PORE   jerod23@well.sf.ca.us
Zine Reviewer; publisher, Poppin' Zits!

STEPHEN PORTER   CGW@mcimail.com
Editor, Computer Graphics World

JANE PRATt   sassy@phantom.com
Sassy *magazine*

PETER RAFLE   70534.3234@compuserve.com
Trout

BILL RAYL   70007.4640@compuserve.com
CONNECT

TARA REGAN   72360.1250@compuserve.com
Journal of Emergency Medical Service

BRIAN REID   reid@mejac.palo-alto.ca.us
Editor and publisher, The USENET Cookbook

ED RICCIUTI   72500.566@compuserve.com
Connecticut Audubon

LOUIS ROSSETTO   lr@wired.com
Editor, Wired *magazine*

CHIP ROWE   75250.1311@compuserve.com
American Journalism Review

ALAN SANDMAN   70741.333@compuserve.com
ARTLINK

CHARLES SAYERS   72700.3172@compuserve.com
CD Media

KEVIN SHARP   71601.707@compuserve.com
ID Systems *magazine*

JOE SIKORYAK   sik@uworld.com

Art director, UnixWorld

MARK SIMMONS   72511.256@compuserve.com

Associate editor, ZiffNet/Mac

MURRAY SLOVICK   m.slovick@ieee.org

Editor, IEEE Spectrum

K. SONNENLEITER   100063.3631@compuserve.com

FOCUS

VIN SPARANO   76376.563@compuserve.com

Outdoor Life

ALAN SPERLING   71470.2724@compuserve.com

Pondscape *magazine*

LISA STAPLETON   lisas@uworld.com

Products editor, UnixWorld

BRIAN STEFFENS   76330.1376@compuserve.com

The QUILL

STEVE G. STEINBERG   tek@well.sf.ca.us

Editor, Intertek

CHUCK STEWART   73270.2236@compuserve.com

Que

MICHAEL STEWART   72520.2313@compuserve.com

Developer's Insight

MICHAEL STRANGELOVE   441495@acadvm1.uottawa.ca

Editor, The Internet Business Journal

NICHOLAS P. SULLIVAN   76530.523@compuserve.com
Executive editor, Home Office Computing

ED SUSSMAN   70317.410@compuserve.com
National Enquirer

RAY SWARTZ   rays@uworld.com
Contributing editor, UnixWorld

SHEF SYED   72511.75@compuserve.com
Project leader, ZiffNet/Mac

BEN TEMPLIN   72511.35@compuserve.com
Executive editor, ZiffNet/Mac

JOHN THEUNG   theung@unx.com
Product review editor, The X Journal

JIM THOMAS   cudigest@phantom.com
Editor, Computer Underground Digest

TERRY ULICK   72700.567@compuserve.com
Storm

KEVIN VANHOOK   Frost1@aol.com
Editor and vice president, Valiant Comics

TOM WATERS   72350.1764@compuserve.com
Editor, Earth *magazine*

CASPAR WEINBERGER   forbes@phantom.com
Forbes *magazine*

TRACY WEISMAN   70324.343@compuserve.com
Editor, Online Access

between the locust and the tribble in its eating habits... However, my roommate

DON WELK   71510.2353@compuserve.com

Sporting Clays

MATT WELSH   mdw@sunsite.unc.edu

Editor, Linux Doc Project

MICHAEL WESTFORT   westfort@netcom.com

Editor, The Oral Report

RUSTY WESTON   rusty@uworld.com

Features editor, UnixWorld

T'Nika is revolted by this whole discussion, her Vulcan sensibilities being tried

EXPERTS

CECIL ADAMS   ezotti@merle.acns.nwu.edu

Creator of The Straight Dope, *expert on everything*

STEVE BROCK   sbrock@teal.csn.org

Reviewer on alt.books.reviews

DAN BROWN   brown@eff.org

SysAdmin, Electronic Frontier Foundation

ALFREDO DE LA FE   delafe@phantom.com

Communications consultant

CYNTHIA DENTON   cynthia@bigsky.dillon.mt.us

Business teacher via e-mail

JOHN DVORAK   3184192@mcimail.com

Columnist, iconoclast, entrepreneur

ESTHER DYSON   5113763@mcimail.com

Computer guru, publisher

MIKE GODWIN   mnemonic@eff.org

Legal counsel to the Electronic Frontier Foundation

CHRIS LOCKE   clocke@panix.com

Internet World, *pundit, guru*

CRAIG MATTOCKS   craig@nhc-hp0.nhc.noaa.gov

NOAA researcher

GEOFF MILLER   geoff@purplehaze.sun.com

Mr. alt.tasteless 1991

JOE NEAL   djkiller@aol.com

Graphic designer

MARK POWELL   aoml@enh.nist.gov

Hurricane researcher, NOAA

DAVID POWERS   powers@inf.enst.fr

Neural nets expert

JOHN S. QUARTERMAN   jsa@tic.com

Texas Internet Consulting

HEMANT ROTITHOR   hemant@ee.wpi.edu

Computer engineer

PATRICIA TUAMA   rissa@world.std.com

Graphic artist

GOVERNMENT MANDARINS

ACE   ace-mg@esusda.gov
Mail to all ACE members

PAMELA ANDRE   pandre@esusda.gov
Agriculture

LYNN BELLARDO   x11@cu.nih.edu
Archives

DOUG BROWN   dbrown@sun1.wwb.noaa.gov
Commerce

CANADIAN FEDERAL IMMIGRATION
AND REFUGEE BOARD   immrefbr@chicken.planet.org
If you decide to flee to Canada...

CANADIAN HUMAN
RIGHTS COMMISSION   canhumrt@chicken.planet.org

KEVIN CARR   kcarr@micf.nist.gov
Commerce

CENTER FOR
CIVIC NETWORKING   mfidelman@world.std.com

Member, Americans Communicating Electronically

PAUL CHRISTY   kpchristy@esa.doc.gov

Commerce

BILL CLINTON   president@whitehouse.gov

President, U.S.A.

CLINTON ADMINISTRATION   75300.3115@compuserve.com

The President and his staff

CONGRESSIONAL
SUBCOMMITTEE
ON TELECOMMUNICATIONS
AND FINANCE   congress@town.hall.org

DENNIS CONNORS   dconnors@access.digex.net

Commerce

GUS CORONEL   gus@phantom.dot.gov

Transportation

STEVE DOWNS   sdowns@oash.ssw.dhhs.gov

Health and Human Services

PATRYK DRESCHER   drescher@access.digex.net

State Department

ED FITZSIMMONS   fitzsimmons@charm.isi.edu

White House

JACK FOX   jfox@esusda.gov

White House, Office of Administration

JONATHAN GILL   jgill@esusda.gov
White House, Office of Media Affairs

AL GORE   vice.president@whitehouse.gov
Vice president, U.S.A.

GREEN PARTY OF CANADA   green@chicken.planet.org
The environmental voice of Canada

CHRISTOPHER GRONBECK   gronbeck@access.digex.net
Energy

MARY CLARE GUMBLETON   mcgumble@inet.ed.gov
Education

WILLIAM HALL   hall.william@epamail.epa.gov
EPA

LINDA HARRIS   lharris@oash.ssw.dhhs.gov
Health and Human Services

LONN HENRICHSEN   lhenrich@phantom.dot.gov
Transportation

MAT HEYMAN   heyman@micf.nist.gov
Commerce

PETE KNECHT   pknecht@esusda.gov
State Department

FRED S. LONG   long@osi.ncsl.nist.gov
Commerce

DAVID LYTEL   alytel@ostp.eop.gov
White House

CHRIS MACDONALD	cmacdon@esusda.gov

State Department

CHIEF MCCORMACK	mccormac@chicken.planet.org

Head of the Metro Toronto Police

AVRA MICHELSON	tmi@cu.nih.gov

Archives

MINISTER OF AGRICULTURE	agricult@chicken.planet.org

Major cabinet post in Canada

MINISTER OF CONSUMER AND CORPORATE AFFAIRS	consumer@chicken.planet.org

Minor cabinet post in Canada

MINISTER OF FISHERIES/OCEANS	fisherie@chicken.planet.org

Major cabinet post in Canada

MINISTER OF HEALTH AND WELFARE	health@chicken.planet.org

Major cabinet post in Canada

MINISTER OF LABOUR	labour@chicken.planet.org

Major cabinet post in Canada

MINISTER OF NATIONAL REVENUE	revenue@chicken.planet.org

Major cabinet post in Canada

MINISTER OF SUPPLY AND SERVICE	supply@chicken.planet.org

Minor cabinet post in Canada

MINISTER OF
THE ENVIRONMENT   environ@chicken.planet.org

Major cabinet post in Canada

MINISTER
OF TRANSPORTATION   transpor@chicken.planet.org

Major cabinet post in Canada

THE MORINO FOUNDATION   mmorino@morino.org

Member, Americans Communicating Electronically

NASA HEADLINE NEWS   nasanews@space.mit.edu

The inside scoop on the shuttle

THE NATIONAL INSTITUTES
OF HEALTH CANCERNET   cancernet@icicb.nci.nih.gov

For more information, send a message with help *in the message body.*

NEW DEMOCRATIC
PARTY OF CANADA   ndpcan@chicken.planet.org

One of the major Canadian parties

OFFICE OF
TECHNOLOGY ASSESSMENT   elecdelivery@ota.gov

Member, Americans Communicating Electronically

ONTARIO HUMAN RIGHTS
COMMISSION   onthumrt@chicken.planet.org

GREG PARHAM   gparham@esusda.gov

Agriculture

PAUL PETERS   paul@cni.org

Coalition for Networked Information

mate)

#: 124956 S2/Star Trek 02-May-87 20:53:29 Sb: #124937-

JIM PINKELMAN   jpinkel@esusda.gov

State Department

JANET POLEY   jpoley@esusda.gov

Agriculture

PREMIER OF ONTARIO   ontprem@chicken.planet.org

The head of the richest province in Canada

STAN PROCHASKA   a13sprochaska@attmail.com

Agriculture

KEN ROGERS   krogers@doc.gov

Commerce

KEVIN ROSSEEL   rosseel.kevin@epamail.epa.gov

EPA

JUNE ROWLANDS   rowlands@chicken.planet.org

Mayor of Toronto

TOM SANDMAN   tommys50@attmail.com

Interior

JOHN SCHMIDT   jschmidt@sun1.wwb.noaa.gov

Commerce

GEORGE SHEPHARD   gshephard@esusda.gov

Labor

THE SOCIAL SECURITY ARCHIVE   nfo@soafl.ssa.gov

For more information, send a message with send index *in the message body.*

MIKE STEIN	stein.mike@epamail.epa.gov
EPA	

ANITA STOCKMAN	astock@esusda.gov
State Department	

WILLIAM TAFOYA	foyaorion@arc.nasa.gov
FBI Agent	

VIC TRUNZO	vtrunzo@esusda.gov
Labor	

LISA WEBER	ywe@cu.nih.edu
Archives	

BARBARA WHITE	bwhite@esusda.gov
Agriculture	

CHRISTINE WHITMAN	cwhitman@rutgers.edu
Governor, New Jersey	

AMY WILLIAMS	awilliams@esa.gov
Commerce	

BROCK WOOD	brwood@nyx.cs.du.edu
U.S. attorney	

JANET WRIGHT	jwright@esusda.gov
Agriculture	

PETER YEE	yee@trident.arc.nasa.gov
Posts official NASA news	

JERRY YOUNG	76040.444@compuserve.com
GSA	

give me a break. Just because something is small and furry doesn't necessarily

ICONS AND SEMI- FICTIONAL CHARACTERS

CITY OF TORONTO   toronto@chicken.planet.org

A city with its own e-mail address

SANTA CLAUS   santa@north.pole.org

He knows who's been naughty...

COKE MACHINE   finger drink drink.csh.rit.edu

The first Coke machine on the net

SCOTT FLANSBURG   76450.3164@compuserve.com

The Human Calculator

THE ORACLE   oracle@iuvax.cs.indiana.edu

Send a note with help *as the subject to discover a way-cool program*

METRO TORONTO ZOO   mtzoo@chicken.planet.org

The gorillas write back if you're nice

SANTA'S ELVES   elves@north.pole.org

Santa's helpers

TORONTO BLUE JAYS   bluejays@chicken.planet.org

No longer an oxymoron, a Canadian baseball team

TORONTO MAPLE LEAFS   leafs@chicken.planet.org

The original hockey team, now trying for a comeback

kill them. Then you eat them. Eating a live tarantula can be hazardous to your

INTERNET DENIZENS

VINTON G. CERF   vcerf@CNRI.reston.va.us

Father of the Internet

COMPUTER PROFESSIONALS
FOR SOCIAL RESPONSIBILITY   cspr@csli.stanford.edu

Watchdog organization

CHRISTOPHER CONDON   bitlib@yalevm.ycc.yale.edu

Editor, Bitnet Services Library

THOMAS P. COPLEY   go_pher_it@netcom.com

Gopher guru

DAVID V. ECKER   decker@ic.sunysb.edu

President, Stony Brook Computer Science Society

ELECTRONIC MAIL
ASSOCIATION (EMA)   70007.2377@compuserve.com

TIM GILMAN   tdgilman@ce.berkeley.edu

Subject of alt.flame.tim-gilman

TOM GRUNDNER   aa0011@nptn.org
*Freenet originator; founder NPTN; National Public Telecomputing
Network*

MICHAEL HART   hart@umd.cso.uiuc.edu
Head of Project Gutenberg

BRIAN JOHNSON   Bjohnson@panix.com
Internet Guide

KIBO   kibo@world.std.com
Typeface designer and omnipotent presence

PATRICK K. KROUPA   digital@phantom.com
Internet guru

DAVID LAWRENCE   tal@uunet.uu.net
Usenet News Administrator

JOHN LITTLE   jel@corp.portal.com
Portal Communications

CARL MALAMUD   carl@trystero.malamud.com
Distributor of SEC data by Internet

JIM MCBRIDE   jimm@netmail.com
President JS McBride & Co.; Internet facilitator

CLAUDE ERIK MEYER   cmeyer@nyx.cs.du.edu
Internet guru

JOHN OJEDA   11ojeda@gallua.galluadet.edu
Washington, D.C. BBS organizer

KEITH PETERSEN w8sdz@vela.acs.oakland.edu

Simtel MSDOS archive maintainer

HOWARD RHEINGOLD hlr@well.sf.ca.us

Author of Virtual Reality: Tools for Thought

THOMAS TATE ttate@esusda.gov

Administrator, ACE (Americans Communicating Electronically)

RUSTY WILLIAMS rusty@delphi.com

Major player at Delphi

SCOTT YANOFF yanoff@csd4.csd.uwm.edu

Internet Connection List compiler

But tribbles are small, furry, AND adorable. And they purr. (I think I just

INTERNET
MAILING LISTS

If you really like getting mail, try subscribing to one of these mailing lists. You'll receive the full text of every message posted by each person on the list—hundreds of messages a day for an active list.

To join a list, you must subscribe by sending mail to the address listed below. The first line of your message should contain the text listed below.

78s   listserv@cornell.edu

Music and recordings of the pre-LP era
    SUB 78-L <your real name>

Advanced Electronics   listserv@utfsm.bitnet

The latest advances in electronics
    SUB ADV-ELO <your real name>

Aircraft   listserv@grearn.bitnet

Aircraft and helicopters, modern and old
    SUB AIRCRAFT <your real name>

American Literature   listserv@umcvmb.missouri.edu

From Dreiser to Salinger and beyond
    SUB AMLIT-L <your real name>

Amnesty International   listserv@jhuvm.bitnet
Freedom around the world
   SUBSCRIBE AMNESTY <your real name>

Animal Rights   animal-rights-request@xanth.cs.odu.edu
Animated discussion on both sides
   nothing required in body

Aquarium   listserv@emuvm1.cc.emory.edu
All things related to the hobby of keeping aquariums
   SUBSCRIBE AQUARIUM <your real name>

Art Critics   listserv@yorkvm1.bitnet
For those interested in the visual arts
   SUB ARTCRIT <your real name>

Artificial Life   alife-request@iuvax.cs.indiana.edu
Using computers to create life
   nothing required in body

Audio   listserv@vmtecmex.bitnet
Speaker builders and audiophiles welcome
   SUB AUDIO-L <your real name>

BBS   listserv@saupmoo.bitnet
Starting, using, and maintaining BBSs
   SUBSCRIBE BBS-L <your real name>

Beverly Hills 90210   90210-request@ferkel.ucsb.edu
The empty-headed Fox TV show
   nothing required in body

Blues   listserv@brownvm.brown.edu
Chicago, Texas, old and new
   SUB BLUES-L <your real name>

BMW   bmw-request@sol.crd.ge.com

Discussion of BMW cars
   nothing required in body

Brass   brass-request@geomag.gly.fsu.edu

Trumpets, tubas, and flugelhorns
   nothing required in body

British Cars   british-cars-request@encore.com

Owning, showing, and driving British cars
   nothing required in body

Bruce Springsteen   backstreets-request@virginia.edu

Fans of Bruce Springsteen
   nothing required in body

Buddha   listserv@ulkyvm.louisville.edu

Buddhist studies
   SUBSCRIBE BUDDHA-L <your real name>

Cable TV   catv-request@quack.sac.ca.us.

Any topic having to do with cable television
   nothing required in body

Cavers   cavers-request@m2c.org

For spelunkers
   nothing required in body

Chaucer   listserv@siucvmb.siu.edu

Medieval literature
   SUB CHAUCER <your real name>

Chess   listserv@grearn.bitnet

Play or just kibbitz
   SUB CHESS-L <your real name>

Classic Texts   listserv@uwavm.u.washington.edu
Ancient Greek and Latin subjects
        SUBSCRIBE CLASSICS <your real name>

Classical Music   listserv@brownvm.brown.edu
Bach to Cage
        SUB CLASSM-L <your real name>

Clayart   listserv@ukcc.uky.edu
More than just dancing raisins
        SUB CLAYART <your real name>

Clothing Optional Living   listserv@etsuadmn.bitnet
Where do you keep your car keys?
        SUB CLTHOPT <your real name>

Comix   comix-request@world.std.com
Non-mainstream comic books
        nothing required in body

Derby   derby-request@mips.com
Aspects and strategies of horse racing
        nothing required in body

Dogs   listserv@pccvm.bitnet
Matters of interest to dog owners
        SUB CANINE-L <your real name>

Eclipse   eclipse-request@beach.cis.ufl.edu
Fans of Pink Floyd and spinoff groups
        nothing required in body

Esperanto   listserv@grearn.bitnet
Working toward a world language
        SUB ESPER-L <your real name>

Fiction Writers   writers-request@studguppy.lanl.gov

Support of and discussion by writers
  nothing required in body

Funky Music   funky-music-request@apollo.lap.upenn.edu

Funk, R&B, soul, hip-hop
  nothing required in body

Funnies   funnies-subscribe@list.kean.edu

The passing back and forth of comic sayings, jokes, etc.
  nothing required in body

Go   mailserv%smcvax.bitnet@vm1.nodak.edu

The ancient Oriental game
  SUBSRIBE GO-L <your real name>

Grateful Dead   dead-flames-request@virginia.edu

Driving that train...
  nothing required in body

Green Organizations   listserv@indyvax.bitnet

Environmental organizations
  SUB GREENORG <your real name>

Hey Joe   hey-joe-request@ms.uky.edu

Worship of Jimi Hendrix
  nothing required in body

Homebrew   homebrew-request%hpfcmr@hplabs.hp.com

Brew-it-yourself
  nothing required in body

Horse   horse-request@bbn.com

Things equestrian
  nothing required in body

distant relatives of true cats...which of course, are related to the wonderful

Humor   listserv@uga.cc.uga.edu

Humor of all types, topics, and tastes
    SUB HUMOR <your real name>

In-My-Life   listserv@wkuvx1.bitnet

Beatles-era popular culture
    SUB INMYLIFE <your real name>

Italian Cars   italian-cars-request@sol.crd.ge.com

Broken or working
    nothing required in body

Jane's Addiction   janes-addiction-request@ms.uky.edu

Fans of Jane's Addiction
    nothing required in body

Japanese Food
          listserv%jpnknu10.bitnet@cunyvm.cuny.edu

Do you put avocado in your hamachi?
    SUB J-FOOD-L <your real name>

Kites   kites-request@harvard.harvard.edu

Making and flying kites
    nothing required in body

Lacrosse   listserv@villvm.bitnet

Big sticks and hard heads
    SUB LACROS-L <your real name>

Libertarians   libernet-request@dartmouth.edu

Laissez Faire pro and con
    nothing required in body

List of Mailing Lists   mail-men-request@attunix.att.com

Keep abreast of active mailing lists
    nothing required in body

Schrodingers cats of Heinlein's "Cat who Walked through Walls" fame. Bill

Magic   magic-request@crdgwl.ge.com

Sleight of hand and the art of magic
nothing required in body

Martial Arts   martial-arts-request@dragon.cso.uiuc.edu

The martial arts
nothing required in body

Miles Davis   listserv@hearn.bitnet

Bitches Brew
SUBSCRIBE MILES <your real name>

MTV Cybersleaze   cyber-sleaze-request@mtv.com

Insight and analysis of the genre
*subscribe CYBER-SLEAZE _your email address_*

Musicals   musicals-request@world.std.com

Movie and stage musicals
nothing required in body

Mystery   mystery-request@csd4.csd.uwm.edu

The butler did it
nothing required in body

Net Surfing   listserv%vmtecmex.bitnet@cunyvm.cuny.edu

Information about Servers, FTP sites, etc.
SUB NETSCOUT <your real name>

Opera   mailserv%brfapesp.bitnet@vm1.nodak.edu

Fat people singing loudly
SUBSCRIBE OPERA-L <your real name>

Origami   origami-l-request@nstn.ns.ca

All facets of the Japanese art of paper folding
nothing required in body

Pagan Religions   pagan-request@drycas.club.cc.cmu.edu

Issues and discussions for pagans
    nothing required in body

Peace Corps   listserv@cmuvm.csv.cmich.edu

Issues involving the Peace Corps
    SUBSCRIBE PCORPS-L <your real name>

Rolling Stones
    undercover-request@snowhite.cis.uoguelph.ca

You can't always get what you want...
    nothing required in body

Rubik's Cube   cube-lovers-request@ai.ai.mit.edu

Twist and turn until you see the right answer
    nothing required in body

SciFi   sf-lovers-request@rutgers.edu

Anything science fiction
    nothing required in body

Sports Cards   cards-request@tanstaafl.uchicago.edu

Collection of and investing in sports cards
    nothing required in body

Star Trek Reviews   listserv@cornell.edu

A noise-free forum for reviews of Star Trek material
    SUBSCRIBE TREK-REVIEW-L <your real name>

Super Nintendo   snes-request@spcvxa.spc.edu

The inside scoop on Starfox
    nothing required in body

Toronto Blue Jays   jays-request@hivnet.ubc.ca

Fans of the Toronto Blue Jays baseball team
    nothing required in body

U2   grace@delphi.com

Fans of Bono, The Edge, Adam & Larry
    nothing required in body

United Nations   listserv@indycms.iupui.edu

Issues involving the United Nations
    SUB UN <your real name>

Usenet Oracle   oracle@iuvax.cs.indiana.edu

Available to answer all your questions
    HELP in subject line

Vegetarians   listserv%gitvm1.bitnet@cunyvm.cuny.edu

No pigs.
    SUB GRANOLA <your real name>

MANUFACTURER SUPPORT ONLINE

AATRIX SOFTWARE   aatrix@aol.com
_____

ACCESS SOFTWARE   links@aol.com
_____

ACTIVISION   activision@aol.com
_____

ADVANCED SOFTWARE   advanced@aol.com
_____

AFFINITY MICROSYSTEMS   affinity@aol.com
_____

ALADDIN SYSTEMS   aladdin@aol.com
_____

ALTSYS CORP.	altsys@aol.com
ALYSIS SOFTWARE	alysis@aol.com
APPLE COMPUTER	apple.bugs@applelink.apple.com
For reporting bugs	
APPLIED ENGINEERING	ae@aol.com
ARGOSY	argosy@aol.com
ARIEL PUBLISHING	ariel@aol.com
ARTICULATE SYSTEMS	asi@aol.com
BASELINE PUBLISHING	baseline@aol.com
BEAGLE BROTHERS	beaglebros@aol.com
BERKELEY SOFTWORKS	berkeley@aol.com
BERKELEY SYSTEMS	berksys@aol.com
BIOSCAN	bioscan@aol.com

BLOC PUBLISHING	bloc@aol.com
BOWERS DEVELOPMENT	bowers@aol.com
BRODERBUND	broderbund@aol.com
BYTE WORKS	byteworks@aol.com
CE SOFTWARE	cesoftware@aol.com
CLARINET INFORMATION	info@clarinet.com
CLARIS	claris@aol.com
CONNECTIX	connectix@applelink.apple.com
COSTAR	costar@aol.com
CULTURAL RESOURCES	cultural@aol.com
DACEASY, INC.	daceasy@aol.com
DAVIDSON & ASSOCIATES	davidson@aol.com

DAYNA COMMUNICATIONS	dayna@aol.com
DIGITAL VISION	digital@aol.com
DIRECT SOFTWARE	direct@aol.com
DOVE COMPUTER	dove@aol.com
DUBL-CLICK SOFTWARE	dublclick@aol.com
ELECTRIC IMAGE	electric@aol.com
ELECTRONIC FRONTIER FOUNDATION	eff@eff.org
ELENAY CREATIONS SOFTWARE	elenay@aol.com
EMIGRE FONTS	emigre@aol.com
FARALLON	farallon@aol.com
FIFTH GENERATION	fifth@aol.com
FONTBANK	fontbank@aol.com

FREE SOFTWARE FOUNDATION	gnu@prep.ai.mit.edu
GATEWAY	72662.163@compuserve.com
GATEWAY	72662.164@compuserve.com
GATEWAY	75300.1300@compuserve.com
GCC TECHNOLOGIES	gcc@aol.com
GEOWORKS	geoworks@aol.com
GLOBAL VILLAGE COMMUNICATION	global@aol.com
GRAPHISOFT	graphisoft@aol.com
INFOCOM	infocom@aol.com
INLINE DESIGN	inline@aol.com
KENT MARSH	kentmarsh@aol.com
KIWI SOFTWARE	kiwi@aol.com

KOALA	macvision@aol.com
LANGUAGE SYSTEMS	languagesys@aol.com
LEADING EDGE INFORMATION	leadingedge@aol.com
LEAGUE FOR PROGRAMMING FREEDOM	league@prep.ai.mit.edu
LETRASET	letraset@aol.com
LUCASFILM GAMES	lucasfilm@aol.com
MACARTIST	macartist@aol.com
MACAVENUE	macavenue@aol.com
MACROMIND	macromind@aol.com
MARKET MASTER	market@aol.com
MARKETFIELD SOFTWARE	marketfield@aol.com

MAXIS	maxis@aol.com
MECC	mecc@aol.com
MERIDIAN DATA	meridian@aol.com
MICRO DYNAMICS	microdynamics@aol.com
MICROCOM	microcom@aol.com
MICROMAT COMPUTER SYSTEMS	micromat@aol.com
MICRON TECHNOLOGY	micron@aol.com
MICROPROSE	microprose@aol.com
MICROSEEDS PUBLISHING	microseeds@aol.com
MICROSOFT	microsoft@aol.com
MILLIKEN	milliken@aol.com
MIRROR TECHNOLOGIES	mirror@aol.com

NATIONAL RESEARCH & EDUCATION NETWORK	nren-discuss@uu.psi.com
NEW ERA	newera@aol.com
NOW SOFTWARE	now@aol.com
OBJECT FACTORY	objectfactory@aol.com
ON TECHNOLOGY	on@aol.com
OPTIMAGE INTERACTIVE SERVICES	optimage@aol.com
PERSONAL COMPUTER PERIPHERALS	pcpc@aol.com
PETER NORTON COMPUTING	symantec@aol.com
POLITICAL ACTION	70750.342@compuserve.com
PORTFOLIO SYSTEMS	dyno@aol.com
POWER UP SOFTWARE	powerup@aol.com

PROVUE DEVELOPMENT	provue@aol.com
QUARK	quark@aol.com
SALIENT SOFTWARE	salient@aol.com
SHIVA CORPORATION	shiva@aol.com
SIERRA ON-LINE	sierra@aol.com
SOFTEK DESIGN	softek@aol.com
SOFTSYNC	softsync@aol.com
SOLUTIONS, INC.	solutions@aol.com
SPECTRUM HOLOBYTE	spectrum@aol.com
SPECULAR INTERNATIONAL	specular@aol.com
SSSI	sssi@aol.com
STRATA	strata@aol.com

STRATEGIC SIMULATIONS	ssi@aol.com
SUPERMAC	supermac@aol.com
SYMANTEC	symantec@aol.com
T/MAKER	tmaker@aol.com
TACTIC SOFTWARE	tactic@aol.com
TECHNOLOGY WORKS	techworks@aol.com
TGS SYSTEMS	tgs@aol.com
VIRTUS	virtus@aol.com
THE VOYAGER COMPANY	voyager@aol.com
WORDPERFECT	wordperfect@aol.com
WORKING SOFTWARE	working@aol.com
ZEDCOR	zedcor@aol.com

MEDIA
OUTLETS

AEROSPACE DAILY   pa93-21@darpa.mil

Voice of the aerospace industry

BOSTON GLOBE   voxbox@globe.com

Regular column on cyberspace

CANADIAN BROADCASTING
CORPORATION (CBC)   cbc@chicken.planet.org

The major television network in Canada

EYE WEEKLY   eye@chicken.planet.org

JOHN GILES   gilestv@echonyc.com

Videographer

GLOBAL TELEVISION
NETWORK   global@chicken.planet.org

Canadian television network

JOE HARRIS   midx@aol.com

Administrative contact, NBC e-mail

THE INDEPENDENT
COMPUTER PAGE   comppage@independent.co.uk

A London newspaper

LAW OFFICE TECHNOLOGY REVIEW   bbayer@bix.com

Just what it says

MACWEEK MAGAZINE   macweek@applelink.apple.com

The best magazine for Mac users

MEDIA PAGE   mpage@phantom.com

News service

THE MIDDLESEX NEWS   sysop@news.ci.net

Paper in Massachusetts

MORNING JOURNAL   mamjornl@freenet.lorain.oberlin.edu

Paper in Lorain, Ohio

NOW MAGAZINE   now@chicken.planet.org

Canadian journal

OTTAWA CITIZEN   ottawa-citizen@freenet.carleton.ca

Paper in Ottawa

MARIANNE PETIT   petit@echonyc.com

Videographer

SANTA CRUZ COUNTY SENTINEL   sented@cruzio.com

Paper in California

ST. PETERSBURG TIMES   73174.3344@compuserve.com

Paper in Florida

Trek 02-May-87 21:58:01 Sb: #124776-#Tribblemania, Fm: Audrey II

THE SEATTLE TIMES	edtimes@hebron.connected.com

Seattle's paper

TICO TIMES	ttimes@huracon.cr

Newspaper in Costa Rica

TORONTO GLOBE AND MAIL	globe@chicken.planet.org

The New York Times *of Canada*

TORONTO STAR	torstar@chicken.planet.org

Leading Canadian metro newspaper

TORONTO SUN	torsun@chicken.planet.org

Canadian tabloid

XTRA!	xtra@chicken.planet.org

NEWS GROUP MODERATORS

NOTE: News groups are the hubs of the Internet, the place where like-minded folk can find each other. Send e-mail to a moderator for details on the list or to get the straight dope on a topic.

ALT.FAN.WARLORD	gmcquary@sequent.com
George F. McQuary	
ALT.GOURMAND	recipes-request@decwrl.dec.com
Brian Reid	
BIONET.SOFTWARE.SOURCES	software-sources@genbank.bio.net
Eliot Lear	
BIT.LISTSERV.BIG-LAN	big-mod@suvm.acs.syr.edu
John Wobus	
BIT.LISTSERV.EDTECH	21765eddt%msu@cunyvm.cuny.edu
Group on educational technology	
BIT.LISTSERV.GAYNET	gaynet-request@athena.mit.edu
Bill Cattey	

BIT.LISTSERV.HELLAS	alex@auvm.american.edu

Alexandros Couloumbis

BIT.LISTSERV.L-HCAP	wtm@bunker.shel.isc-br.com

Bill McGarry

BIT.LISTSERV.NEW-LIST	info@vm1.nodak.edu

Marty Hoag

BIT.LISTSERV. PACS-L	libpacs%uhupvm1@cunyvm.cuny.edu

Charles Bailey

BIT.LISTSERV.VALET-L	krvw@cert.sei.cmu.edu

Kenneth van Wyk

COMP.AI.NLANG-KNOW-REP	nl-kr-request@cs.rpi.edu

Christopher Welty

COMP.AI.VISION	vision-list-request@ads.com

Tod Levitt

COMP.ARCHIVES	comp-archives@msen.com

Edward Vielmetti

COMP.BINARIES.ACORN	moderator@acorn.co.uk

Alan Glover

COMP.BINARIES.AMIGA	amiga-request@uunet.uu.net

Tad Guy

COMP.BINARIES. ATARI.ST	atari-binaries@twitterpater.eng.sun.com

Steven Grimm

COMP.BINARIES.
IBM.PC   ibmbin-request@crdgwl.crd.ge.com

Bill Davidsen

COMP.BINARIES.
MAC   macintosh-request%felix.uucp@uunet.uu.net

Roger Long

COMP.BINARIES.OS2   os2bin-request@csd4.csd.uwm.edu

Michael D. Kretzer

COMP.BUGS.4BSD.
UCB-FIXES   ucb-fixes-request@okeeffe.berkeley.edu

Keith Bostic

COMP.
COMPILERS   compilers-request@iecc.cambridge.ma.us

John Levine

COMP.DCOM.TELECOM   telecom-request@eecs.nwu.edu

Patrick Townson

COMP.DOC   comp-doc@ucsd.edu

Brian Kantor

COMP.DOC.TECHREPORTS
                 compdoc-techreports-request@ftp.cse.ucsc.edu

Richard Golding

COMP.GRAPHICS.
RESEARCH   graphics-request@scril.scri.fsu.edu

John R. Murray

COMP.LANG.SIGPLAN   sigplan-request@bellcore.com

Stu Feldman

| COMP.LASER-PRINTERS | furuta@cs.umd.edu |

Richard Furuta

| COMP.MAIL.MAPS | uucpmap@rutgers.edu |

Mel Pleasant

| COMP.NEWPROD | newprod-request@chg.mcd.mot.com |

Ron Heiby

| COMP.ORG.FIDONET | pozar@hop.toad.com |

Tim Pozar

| COMP.OS.RESEARCH | darrell@cse.ucsc.edu |

Darrell Long

| COMP.PARALLEL | hypercube-request@hubcap.clemson.edu |

Dennis Stevenson

| COMP.PATENTS | pjt@cs.su.oz.au |

Peter John Treloar

| COMP.PROTOCOLS.
KERMIT | info-kermit-request@watsun.cc.columbia.edu |

Frank da Cruz

| COMP.RESEARCH.JAPAN | rick@cs.arizona.edu |

Rick Schlichting

| COMP.RISKS | risks-request@csl.sri.com |

Peter G. Neumann

| COMP.
SIMULATION | simulation-request@uflorida.cis.ufl.edu |

Paul A. Fishwick

COMP.SOCIETY	socicom@auvm.american.edu
Greg Welsh	

COMP.SOCIETY.FOLKLORE	eric@snark.thyrsus.com
Eric Raymond	

COMP.SOURCES.3B1	dave@galaxia.newport.ri.us
David H. Brierley	

COMP.SOURCES.ACORN	moderator@acorn.co.uk
Alan Glover	

COMP.SOURCES.AMIGA	amiga-request@uunet.uu.net
Tad Guy	

COMP.SOURCES.APPLE2	jac@paul.rutgers.edu
Jonathan Chandross	

COMP.SOURCES.ATARI.ST	atari-sources@twitterpater.eng.sun.com
Steven Grimm	

COMP.SOURCES.GAMES	games-request@saab.cna.tek.com
Bill Randle	

COMP.SOURCES.HP48	spell@seq.uncwil.edu
Chris Spell	

COMP.SOURCES.MAC	macintosh-request%felix.uucp@uunet.uu.net
Roger Long	

COMP.SOURCES.MISC	sources-misc-request@uunet.uu.net
Kent Landfield	

body didn't come up with that one before *I* did!

#: 124938 S2/Star Trek 02-

| COMP.SOURCES.REVIEWED | csr@calvin.doc.ca |

Andrew Patrick

| COMP.SOURCES.SUN | mcgrew@aramis.rutgers.edu |

Charles McGrew

| COMP.SOURCES.
UNIX | unix-sources-moderator@pa.dec.com |

Paul Vixie, Mike Stump, Nick Lai

| COMP.SOURCES.X | x-sources-request@msi.com |

David C. Martin

| COMP.STD.ANNOUNCE | klensin@infoods.mit.edu |

John C. Klensin

| COMP.STD.MUMPS | std-mumps-request@plus5.com |

Newsgroup on mumps

| COMP.STD.UNIX | std-unix-request@uunet.uu.net |

Sean Eric Fagan

| COMP.SYS.AMIGA.ANNOUNCE | zerkle@cs.ucdavis.edu |

Dan Zerkle

| COMP.SYS.AMIGA.REVIEWS | honp9@menudo.uh.edu |

Jason Tibbitts III

| COMP.SYS.
CONCURRENT | concurrent-request@cortex.neusc.bcm.tmc.edu |

Stan Barber

| COMP.SYS.IBM.
PC.DIGEST | info-ibmpc-request@simtel20.army.mil |

Gregory Hicks

COMP.SYS.M68K.PC   info-68k-request@ucbvax.berkeley.edu

Mike Meyer

COMP.SYS.MAC.ANNOUNCE   werner@rascal.ics.utexas.edu

Werner Uhrig

COMP.SYS.MAC.
DIGEST   info-mac-request@sumex-aim.stanford.edu

Lance Nakata, Jon Pugh, Dwayne Virnau

COMP.SYS.NEXT.
ANNOUNCE   csn-announce-request@media.mit.edu

Pascal Chesnais

COMP.SYS.SUN   sun-spots-request@rice.edu

Robert D. Greene

COMP.THEORY.INFO-RETRIEVAL   engle@cmsa.berkeley.edu

Newsgroup on information retrieval theory

COMP.VIRUS   krvw@cert.sei.cmu.edu

Kenneth van Wyk

GNU.*   info-gnu-request@prep.ai.mit.edu

Leonard H. Tower, Jr.

IEEE.ANNOUNCE   burt@ieee.org

Burt Juda

MISC.ACTIVISM.
PROGRESSIVE   map-request@pencil.cs.missouri.edu

Rich Winkel

MISC.HANDICAP   wtm@bunker.shel.isc-br.com

Bill McGarry

MISC.NEWS.SOUTHASIA   surekha@isis.cs.du.edu
Surekha Gaddam

MISC.SECURITY   security-request@rutgers.edu
A. Walker

NEWS.ANNOUNCE.CONFERENCES   denny@tekbspa.tss.com
Dennis Page

NEWS.ANNOUNCE.IMPORTANT   announce@stargate.com
Mark Horton

NEWS.ANNOUNCE.NEWGROUPS   tale@rpi.edu
David Lawrence

NEWS.ANNOUNCE.NEWUSERS   spaf@purdue.edu
Gene Spafford

NEWS.ANSWERS   news-answers-request@mit.edu
Jonathan I. Kamens

NEWS.LISTS   news-lists-request@cs.purdue.edu
Rick Adams, Brian Reid, Gene Spafford

NEWS.LISTS.PS-MAPS   reid@decwrl.dec.com
Brian Reid

REC.ARTS.CINEMA   thakur@zerkalo.harvard.edu
Manavendra Thakur

REC.ARTS.EROTICA   erotica@telly.on.ca
Evan Leibovitch

REC.ARTS.MOVIES.REVIEWS   movies-request@mtgzy.att.com
Evelyn C. Leeper

REC.ARTS.SF.ANNOUNCE	scott@zorch.sf-bay.org

Scott Hazen Mueller

REC.ARTS.SF.REVIEWS	sf-reviews@presto.ig.com

Michael Berch, Daniel Danehy-Oakes, Evelyn Leeper, Wayne Throop,
Alan Wexelblat, Bill Wisner

REC.ARTS. STARTREK.INFO	trek-info-request@dweeb.fx.com

Jim Griffith

REC.AUDIO. HIGH-END	info-high-audio-request@csd4.csd.uwm.edu

Thomas Krueger

REC.FOOD.RECIPES	aem@mthvax.cs.miami.edu

Andrew Mossberg

REC.GUNS	gun-control@flubber.cs.umd.edu

John Purtilo

REC.HUMOR.FUNNY	funny-request@looking.on.ca

Brad Templeton

REC.HUNTING	hunting-request@osnome.che.wisc.edu

Tim Rigg

REC.MAG.FSFNET	white@duvm.bitnet

John White

REC.MUSIC.GAFFA	love-hounds-request@eddie.mit.edu

Bill Wisner

REC.MUSIC.REVIEWS	stewart@sco.com

Stewart Evans

| SCI.MATH.RESEARCH | dan@math.uiuc.edu |

Daniel R. Grayson

| SCI.MED.AIDS | aids-request@cs.ucla.edu |

Dan Greening

| SCI.MILITARY | military-request@att.att.com |

Bill Thacker

| SCI.NANOTECH | josh@aramis.rutgers.edu |

J. Storrs Hall

| SCI.PSYCHOLOGY.
DIGEST | psyc-request@phoenix.princeton.edu |

Stevan Harnad

SCI.VIRTUAL-WORLDS
virtual-worlds-request@milton.u.washington.edu

Bob Jacobson

| SOC.FEMINISM | feminism-request@ncar.ucar.edu |

Jean Marie Diaz, Miriam Nadel, Cindy Tittle

| SOC.POLITICS | poli-sci-request@rutgers.edu |

Charles McGrew

| SOC.POLITICS.ARMS-D | arms-d-request@xx.lcs.mit.edu |

Herb Lin

| SOC.RELIGION.CHRISTIAN | christian-request@aramis.rutgers.edu |

Charles Hedrick

| SOC.RELIGION.EASTERN | prabhu@amelia.nas.nasa.gov |

Dinesh Prabhu

SOC.RELIGION.ISLAM   religion-islam-request@ncar.ucar.edu

Naim Abdullah, Benham Sadeghi, Shari VanderSpek

VMSNET.ANNOUNCE.NEWUSERS   tp@mccall.com

Terry Poot

VMSNET.SOURCES   vmsnet-sources-request@mvb.saic.com

Mark Berryman

PHILOSOPHERS AND DEEP THINKERS

RALPH ABRAHAM   abraham@cats.ucsc.edu

Research in complex dynamical systems

THOMAS BEVER   bever@prodigal.psych.rochester.edu

Psychologist, left/right brain studies

NOAM CHOMSKY   chomsky@athena.mit.edu

Linguist, philosopher, creator of controversy

CRAIG COCKBURN   craig@scot.demon.co.uk

Director, Gaelic Learner's Association

ROY DYCKHOFF   rd@cs.st-and.ac.uk

Logician

MICHEL EYTAN   eytan@suzuka.u-strasbg.fr

Logician

DOREEN KIMURA   kimura@uwovax.uwo.ca

Psychologist, brain researcher

GEORGES KLEIBER   kleiber@ushs.u-strasbg.fr

Linguist

YI PAN   pan@hype.cps.udayton.edu

Algorithms researcher

SIMON SABBAGH   sabbagh@site-maisons-alfort.fr

Computational linguist

PAUL SAFFO   psaffo@mcaimail.com

Research fellow, Institute for the Future

CELESTIN SEDOGBO   sedogbo@frcl.bull.fr

Computational linguist

ALAN WEXELBLAT   wex@media.mit.edu

Human interface expert, MIT Media Lab

TERRY WINOGRAD   winograd@cs.stanford.edu

Philosopher/computer scientist

PHYSICISTS

TOM HERBERT	therbert@umiami.ir.miami.edu
Physicist	

VICKI ROBINSON	vjrnts@ritvax.isc.rit.edu
Physicist	

JACK SARFATTI	sarfatti@netcom.com
Controversial physicist	

PROGRAMMERS

AMANDA ABELSON   manda@martigny.ai.mit.edu

Became famous as an 8-year-old HyperCard programmer

GEOFF ADAMS   gadams@eng.umd.edu

Desktop Textures programmer

GREG AHARONIAN   srctran@world.std.com

Noted Ada critic

LEWIS ANDERSON   andersol@server2.health.state.mn.us

Mac shareware author

DAVID ASHLEY   dash@netcom.com

Computer game developer

TOM BANCHOFF   tfb@cs.brown.edu

Famous for work in 4-D graphics

CHARLES BENNETT   chuck@benatong.com

Unix programming expert and software developer

BRIAN BERLINER   brian.berliner@central.sun.com

Cvs source management

GRADY BOOCH   egb@rational.com

Object-oriented analysis and design of software systems

JOHN BRADLEY   bradley@cis.upenn.edu

Xv, X image viewer

MIKE BRENNAN   brennan@boeing.com

Mawk (nawk superset)

GUNTHER BRIZNIEK   brizniek@nova.umd.edu

C-BASE BBS

MICHAEL CASTEEL   mac@unison.com

Mac game programmer

WILLIAM CHIA-WEI CHENG   william@cs.ucla.edu

Tgif (X figure editor)

CHRISTOPHER COUNCIL   meep@mit.edu

Mac game programmer

JOHN CRISTY   cristy@dupont.com

ImageMagick, X image viewer

DAVID A. CURRY   davy@ecn.purdue.edu

Xpostit (X Post-it notes)

JOHN DOWNEY   jmd@cyclone.bt.co.uk

Xvi, vi clone

GEORGE FERGUSON   ferguson@cs.rochester.edu

Xarchie, X interface to archie

JIM FROST   jimf@centerline.com

Xloadimage, X image viewer

DESMOND FULLER   fuller@hlsun.red-cross.org

Unix Associate, American Red Cross

AARON GILES   giles@med.cornell.edu

JPEG View programmer

MICHAEL GLEASON   mgleason@cse.unl.edu

Ncftp (ftp superset)

PETER GUTMANN   pgut1@cs.aukuni.ac.nz

Hpack file archiver

PAUL HAAHR   haahr@kaleida.com

Es shell

DAVID HARRIS   david@pmail.gen.nz

Noted software developer

GUY HARRIS   guy@auspex.com

Unix kernel developer

CLAUDE HEINTZ   76120.1220@compuserve.com

MacLux Pro

RICHARD HESKETH   rlh@ukc.ac.uk

Gspreview, Ghostscript interface

ANDY HOOK   anselm@web.apc.org

Computer game developer

ERIC JOHNFELT   ejohnfel@ic.sunysb.edu

Co-owner, Driven by Design (shareware company)

ROBERT JUNG   robjung@world.std.com

Programmer, ARJ

Audrey II 72767,1071 To: Ilene Schneider 72467,3255 #: 124608 S2/Star

BREWSTER KAHLE   brewster@wais.com

Head of WAIS team

ROD KENNEDY   rod@faceng.anu.edu.au

Ulaw utility programmer

JEFFREY H. KINGSTON   jeff@cs.su.oz.au

Lout

DAVID KORN   dgk@ulysses.att.com

Ksh' Unix shell

KAI KRAUSE   afckai@aol.com

Creator of Kai's Power Tools

STEPHEN KRAUTH   phred@eng.umd.edu

Desktop Textures artist

RODNEY LAI   rlai@netcom.com

Computer game developer

IAIN LEA   iain.lea@erlm.siemens.de

Author of Tin Usenet Newsreader

DAN MCDONALD   dmcdonld|rv08@rvdc.unisys.com

Unisys programmer

LOU MONTULLI   montulli@ukanaix.cc.ukans.edu

LYNX (WWW viewer)

BRAM MOOLENAAR   mool@oce.nl

Vim, vi clone

LANCE NORSKOG   thinman@netcom.com

Sox

JOHN NORSTAD   jln@nwu.edu
Macintosh Disinfectant

JARKKO OIKARINEN   jto@rieska.oulu.fi
Original IRC client

JOHN OUSTERHOUT   ouster@sprite.berkeley.edu
Tcl programming language

MIKE PARKER   mouse@larry.mcrcim.mcgill.edu
Mterm, X terminal emulator

VERN PAXSON   vern@cs.cornell.edu
Flex (lex superset)

MIHA PETERNEL   miha@rsc3.hermes.fi
Commodore emulators

M. FRANÇOIS POTTIER   pottier@clipper.ens.fr
Decor programmer

BYRON RAKITZIS   byron@netapp.com
Rc shell

CHET RAMEY   chet@po.cwru.edu
Cleveland Freenet programmer

JOEL RICHARD   jorichar@ic.sunysb.edu
Wizard at ElendorMUSH MUD

JOHANN RUEGG   hruegg@nyx.cs.du.edu
Intel Unix internals

CRAIG RUFF   cruff@ncar.ucar.edu
Macintosh Tar programmer

JEREMY SAN	jez@argonaut.com

Creator of Starfox video game

ANTHONY SAXTON	elenay_creations@tcs.las-vegas.nv.us

WDEF-Mac programmer

MIKE SCHWARTZ	schwartz@cs.colorado.edu

Author of Netfind

KEN SHIRRIFF	shirriff@sprite.berkeley.edu

Xfractint fractals

BRIAN SMITH	bvsmith@lbl.gov

Xfig (X document figure editor)

SAURO SPERANZA	speranza@cirfid.unibo.it

Suntar programmer

RICHARD STALLMAN	rms@athena.mit.edu

EMACS, gnu; founder, Free Software Foundation

JEFF STROBEL	jstrobel@world.std.com

UULite programmer

VICTOR TAN	victort@ucc.su.oz.au

SpeedyFinder programmer

ANDREW TANENBAUM	st@cs.vu.nl

Minix and Amoeba operating systems

IAN LANCE TAYLOR	ian@airs.com

gnu, UUCP

LINUS TORVALDS	torvalds@klaava.helsinki.fi

Linux

PANOS TSIRGOTIS   panos@cs.colorado.edu

Author of Netfind

ALAN TUCHMAN   a-tuchman@uiuc.edu

Xgopher, X interface to gopher

DENNIS VADURA   dvadura@watdragon.waterloo.edu

Dmake (make superset)

LARRY WALL   lwall@netlabs.com

Author of PERL language

WILL WRIGHT   willw@aol.com

Creator of SimCity

KAZU YANAGIHARA   kazu@applelink.apple.com

Macintosh utility programmer

PHIL ZIMMERMAN   prz@acm.org

PGP Personal Cryptography...banned from US export as a munition

REPORTERS

WENDY E. BETTS   webco@cruzio.com

Children's book reviewer

RICH BLALOCK   73052.414@compuserve.com

Reporter, WVUE-TV, New Orleans

PAULINA BORSOOK   loris@well.sf.cau.us

Freelance writer

DAVID CHURBUCK   dbuck@well.sf.ca.us

Forbes

JULIAN DIBBELL   julian@panix.com

Technology writer, The Village Voice

JASON E. DOZIER   71022.220@compuserve.com

The Indianapolis Entertainer

RAY DUNCAN   duncan @cerf.net

Writer, PC Magazine

JOHN DVORAK   72511.226@compuserve.com

MacUser *columnist*

JAMES EVANS	surf93@well.sf.ca.us

San Francisco Daily

GAIL GABRIEL	73510.1561@compuserve.com

Home Office Computing

SIMSON GARFINKEL	simsong@nextworld.com

Editor, Nextworld; *prolific freelance writer*

DAN GILLMOR	dgillmor@det–freepress.com

Detroit Free Press

CONNIE GUGLIELMO	connie.g@applelink.apple.com

Freelance writer for Wired *and* MacWeek

ANDY IHNATKO	andyi@world.std.com

Columnist, MacUser

MARK KELLNER	kellner@psilink.com

Writer, The Washington Times

SHIRLEY DUGLIN KENNEDY	kenneds@firnvx.firn.edu

Writer, St. Petersburg Times

JOHN MARKOFF	markoff@nyt.com

The New York Times

MICHAEL MILLER	mikeym@well.sf.ca.us

The Wall Street Journal

GARY ANDREW POOLE	garyp@uworld.com

Senior writer, UnixWorld

MARK POTTS   mpotts@access.digex.net

Director of product development at Digital Ink, the Washington Post Co.'s electronic-media subsidiary

JOSH QUITTNER   quit@newsday.com

Newsday

ROBIN RASKIN   374-1474@mcimail.com

PC Magazine

JACK SCHOFIELD   70007.5416@compuserve.com

Computer editor, The Guardian *(London)*

MICHAEL SCHRAGE   schrage@media–lab.media.mit.edu

Chronicler of the information highway

DWIGHT SILVERMAN   `dwight.silverman@chron.com

Writer, Houston Chronicle

STEVE STECKLOW   stecklow@village.com

The Wall Street Journal

TOM STEINERT-THRELKELD   tomhyphen@aol.com

Technology writer, The Dallas Morning News

THOMAS STEWART   thosstew@aol.com

Fortune *magazine*

GUS VENDITTO   72241.42@compuserve.com

Windows Sources

JOEL WEBB   72105.1753@compuserve.com

Link-up

DAVID WOGAHN   dwogahn@delphi.com

Times Mirror

GARY WOLF   gwolf@well.sf.ca.us

Columnist for SF Weekly

CHRISTINA WOOD   76004.3673@compuserve.com

PC World *magazine*

Thailand? Friend of mine in college, before moving back to the states, lived with

SYSOPS

ANDREW BURT   aburt@nyx.cs.du.edu
Champion of freenet access, NYX sysop

BILL FLEET   72731.360@compuserve.com
CompuServe sysop

WALT HOWE   walthowe@delphi.com
Delphi Internet SIG manager

MARSHALL LEVIN   aa839@cleveland.freenet.edu
Cleveland Freenet Internet sysop

JOHN POSTEL   postel@isi.edu
Internet Request for Comments (RFC) referee

SUSAN SHEPHERD   76703.4326@compuserve.com
CompuServe sysop

TECHNICAL GURUS

J. ALLARD   jallard@microsoft.com
Microsoft TCP/IP specialist

OSCAR BROOKS   obrooks@ryker.ksc.nasa.gov
Computer engineer, NASA Kennedy Space Center

PAUL W. CAMPBELL   pawcamp@u.cc.utah.edu
PCMCIA summa cum laude

DON CHRISTENSEN   djc@acuson.com
Computer engineer

RON HUNSINGER   ron.hunsinger@bmug.org
Software engineer for Berkeley Macintosh User's Group (BMUG)

MICHAEL JONES   mtj@sgi.com
Advanced graphics division, Silicon Graphics

BOB METCALF   bob_metcalf@infoworld.com
Developer of Ethernet; publisher, InfoWorld *magazine*

CRAIG PARTRIDGE   craig@fruug.org

Author of Gigabit

MARSHALL T. ROSE   mrose@dbc.mtview.ca.us

SNMP guru

JACK SENDAK   jack.t.sendak@office.wang.com

Professional Internet instructor

MARK SHANKS   shanks@saifr00.ateng.az.honeywell.com

Boeing principal displays engineer

TELEVISION STATIONS

ABC NEWS   abcnews@class.org

Research center for network news

CFMT-TV   cfmttv@chicken.planet.org

Toronto television station

CFTO-TV   cftotv@chicken.planet.org

Major Canadian television station

CITYTV   citytv@chicken.planet.org

Toronto television station

CJOH-TV   ab363@freenet.carleton.ca

Television station in Ottawa

CTV TELEVISION NETWORK   ctv@chicken.planet.org

Canadian television

NBC NEWS   nightly@nbc.com

Network TV news outlet

WCCO-TV   wccotv@mr.net

TV station in Minneapolis (but Mary Richards worked at WJM)

WCVB-TV   wcvb@aol.com

TV station in Boston

WTVF-TV   craig.ownsby@nashville.com

TV station in Nashville

THE MILITARY-
INDUSTRIAL
COMPLEX

RON BAALKE   baalke@kelvin.jpl.nasa.gov

Posts official NASA news

ANDREW HAZELTINE   andy@thomas.ge.com

Administrative contact, General Electric e-mail

DAVE HUGHES   dave@oldcolo.com

Former Pentagon counter insurgency expert

J. WILLIAM KIME   adm.kime/g-c01@cgsmtp.comdt.uscg.mil

Commandant, U.S. Coast Guard

ED NIEHAUS   niehaus@well.sf.ca.us

PR, Hughes Corporation

KAREN NOVAK   knovak@usr.com

PR Director, US Robotics

DICK SAINT PETERS   stpeters@bird.crd.ge.com

General Electric

GENERAL ALONZO SHORT   shorta@karpeles.ims.disa.mil

Head, Defense Information Systems Agency

DAVE SILL   de5@ornl.gov

Martin Marietta Energy Systems Workstation support

DAVID SORRELLS   dsorrell@nyx.cs.du.edu

Instructor, Defense Visual Information School, USAF

ROBERT STEELE   steeler@well.sf.ca.us

Former CIA agent

THE RICHEST
AMERICANS
WITH E-MAIL

BILL GATES   billg@microsoft.com

America's wealthiest entrepreneur

ROSS PEROT   71511.460@compuserve.com

Computer executive, failed presidential candidate

USEFUL
ONLINE
SERVICES

AMERICANS
COMMUNICATING ELECTRONICALLY   info@ace.esusda.gov

To request the ACE Vision Statement

NATIONAL PUBLIC
TELECOMPUTING NETWORK   tmg@nptn.org

Member, Americans Communicating Electronically

ONLINE CAREER CENTER   occ@msen.com

Send a note for info on finding a job

RECORDING FOR THE BLIND   cbfb_gwk@selway.umt.edu

Access to books on tape

UNIQUE IMAGES   wave@media.mit.edu

The media lab makes cool pictures

VIRTUAL
REALITY
EXPERTS

KAREN AUGUST   kaugust@caip.rutgers.edu
President, Virtual Reality Alliance of Students and Professionals

Dana Ballard   dana@cs.rochester.edu
Virtual reality researcher

RALF HELBING   helbing@engin.umich.edu
Researcher, Advanced Virtual Reality Lab, University of Michigan

JOAN VAN TASSEL   Jvantass@pepperdine.edu
Assistant professor, Pepperdine University

WORLD PEACE CREATORS (FAR TOO FEW)

TOUKAN ABDULLAH   76347.462@compuserve.com

Second-in-command, Jordan; Jordan & Israel peace negotiator

Gerrold 70307,544 To: Ilene Schneider 72467,3255 (X) Tribbles are actually

ALPHABETICAL LISTING OF NAMES

Aatrix Software ....aatrix@aol.com
ABC News ....abcnews@class.org
Abdullah, Toukan ....76347.462@compuserve.com
Abelson, Amanda ....manda@martigny.ai.mit.edu
Abelson, Hal ....hal@martigny.ai.mit.edu
Abraham, Ralph ....abraham@cats.ucsc.edu
Access Software ....links@aol.com
ACE ....ace-mg@esusda.gov
Activision ....activision@aol.com
Adamec, Chris ....71216.105@compuserve.com
Adams, Cecil ....ezotti@merle.acns.nwu.edu
Adams, Douglas ....76206.2507@compuserve.com
Adams, Geoff ....gadams@eng.umd.edu
Adams, Scott ....scottadams@aol.com
Advanced Software ....advanced@aol.com
Aerospace Daily ....pa93-21@darpa.mil
Affinity Microsystems ....affinity@aol.com
Agre, Phil ....pagre@ucsd.edu
Aharonian, Greg ....srctran@world.std.com
Aladdin Systems ....aladdin@aol.com
Albiston, Doreen ....dalbisto@hr.house.gov
Allard, J ....jallard@microsoft.com
alt.fan.warlord ....gmcquary@sequent.com
alt.gourmand ....recipes-request@decwrl.dec.com
Altsys Corp. ....altsys@aol.com
Alysis Software ....alysis@aol.com
America Online ....@aol.com
Americans Communicating Electronically ....info@ace.esusda.gov
Anbinder, Mike ....mha@baka.ithaca.ny.us
Anderson, Brett ....76646.3722@compuserve.com
Anderson, Lewis ....andersol@server2.health.state.mn.us
Andre, Pamela ....pandre@esusda.gov
Angelis, Pam ....angelis@genie.geis.com
Angell, David ....dangell@shell.portal.com
Apple Computer ....apple.bugs@applelink.apple.com

115

Applelink ....@applelink.apple.com
Applied Engineering ....ae@aol.com
Argosy ....argosy@aol.com
Ariel Publishing...ariel@aol.com
Articulate Systems...asi@aol.com
Ashby, Erin ....75570.2561@compuserve.com
Ashley, David ....dash@netcom.com
Asner, Edward...................................72726.357@compuserve.com
Aspirin, Robert...................................76254.523@compuserve.com
ATTMail...@attmail.com
Aufiero, Ron ....raufiero@hr.house.gov
August, Karen.......................................kaugust@caip.rutgers.edu
Avro, Tom ....73330.1335@compuserve.com
Azzara, Mike...mikea@ost.com
Baalke, Ron ....baalke@kelvin.jpl.nasa.gov
Ballard, Dana ....dana@cs.rochester.edu
Banchoff, Tom..tfb@cs.brown.edu
Banks, John..................................71234.637@compuserve.com
Barlow, John Perry..Barlow@eff.org
Barrett, Don....................................72253.2172@compuserve.com
Barrie, Niki ....74756.445@compuserve.com
Barry, Dave ....73314.722@compuserve.com
Bartell, Mike ....mike_bartell@scc.senate.gov
Bartimole, John.................................71041.3310@compuserve.com
Bartlett, Richard D. ....73374.1107@compuserve.com
Baseline Publishing...baseline@aol.com
Beagle Brothers...beaglebros@aol.com
Bearnson, Lisa..................................76004.3617@compuserve.com
Beavis...beavis@mtv.com
Belcher, Jack ....jbelcher@hr.house.gov
Bell, Douglas...dougbell@netcom.com
Bellardo, Lynn ....x11@cu.nih.edu
Bennett, Alex..abennett@netcom.com
Bennett, Charles ....chuck@benatong.com
Berardinelli, James ....blake7@cc.bellcore.com
Berkeley, Busby...BusbyBrkly@aol.com
Berkeley Softworks...berkeley@aol.com
Berkeley Systems..berksys@aol.com
Berliner, Brian ....brian.berliner@central.sun.com
Best Brains, Inc. ....bbrains@mr.net
Betts, Wendy E. ....webco@cruzio.com
Bever, Thomas.......................bever@prodigal.psych.rochester.edu
Biehl, Allen ....76004.3620@compuserve.com
bionet.software.sources.........................software-sources@genbank.bio.net
BioScan ....bioscan@aol.com
bit.listserv.big-lan ....big-mod@suvm.acs.syr.edu
bit.listserv.edtech ....21765eddt%msu@cunyvm.cuny.edu
bit.listserv.gaynet ....gaynet-request@athena.mit.edu
bit.listserv.hellas ....alex@auvm.american.edu
bit.listserv.l-hcap ....wtm@bunker.shel.isc-br.com
bit.listserv.new-list ....info@vm1.nodak.edu
bit.listserv.pacs-l...........................libpacs%uhupvm1@cunyvm.cuny.edu
bit.listserv.valet-l.................................krvw@cert.sei.cmu.edu
BIX ....@dcibix.das.net
Blagojevic, Bonnie ....BonnieB@maine.maine.edu
Blake, Ted...tblake@hr.house.gov
Blankenhorn, David C. ....dblanken@snm.com
Blinn, Bill ....74365.1543@compuserve.com
BLOC Publishing..bloc@aol.com
Boam, Bryan ....bryan.boam@mhz.com

Booch, Grady..egb@rational.com
Boos, Tom...tcb@pdm4340.cpg.cdc.com
Borsook, Paulina ....loris@well.sf.cau.us
Boston Globe...voxbox@globe.com
Bowers Development ....bowers@aol.com
Bradley, John ....bradley@cis.upenn.edu
Brady, Jordan ....73112.731@compuserve.com
Branden, Nathaniel.......................................73117.607@compuserve.com
Branscum, Deborah..branscum@aol.com
Branwyn, Gareth..gareth2@aol.com
Brennan, Mike ....brennan@boeing.com
Bridgewater, Gary...gbridge@charm.isi.edu
Brizniek, Gunther ....brizniek@nova.umd.edu
Broadhead, Rick..ysar1111@vm1.yorku.ca
Broadhurst, Judith ....70421.2063@compuserve.com
Brock, Steve...sbrock@teal.csn.org
Broderbund ....broderbund@aol.com
Brokaw, Tom..nightly@nbc.com
Broker, Jim ....70717.1343@compuserve.com
Brooks, James L. ....72700.2062@compuserve.com
Brooks, Oscar ....obrooks@ryker.ksc.nasa.gov
Brown, Dan ....brown@eff.org
Brown, Doug...................................dbrown@sun1.wwb.noaa.gov
Browning, John ....browning@well.sf.ca.us
Buchanan, Pat..76326.126@compuserve.com
Buford, Mark ....nvmxb02@nt.com
Bunch, Chris..73354.3157@compuserve.com
Burgard, Michael ....mikeb@uworld.com
Burgess, Buck...lburgess@hr.house.gov
Burk, Ron..ronb@rdpub.com
Burt, Andrew...aburt@nyx.cs.du.edu
Burton, Jim...75300.2316@compuserve.com
Butthead..butthead@mtv.com
Byte Works ....byteworks@aol.com
Cameron, Bruce ....71171.1344@compuserve.com
Cammy, Neal..70431.3102@compuserve.com
Campanell, Robert ....robcamp@seas.gwu.edu
Campbell, Paul W..pawcamp@u.cc.utah.edu
Canadian Broadcasting Corporation (CBC)...........cbc@chicken.planet.org
Canadian Federal Immigration and Refugee Board...................................
....immrefbr@chicken.planet.org
Canadian Human Rights Commission ....canhumrt@chicken.planet.org
Card, Orson Scott....................................70044.3107@compuserve.com
Cargill, Tom ....cargill@fruug.org
Carr, Kevin ....kcarr@micf.nist.gov
Carroll, Jim..jcarroll@jacc.com
Carroll, Roger ....72212.1002@compuserve.com
Carroll, T...71550.133@compuserve.com
Casey, Chris..ccasey@hr.house.gov
Casteel, Michael ....mac@unison.com
CE Software...cesoftware@aol.com
Center for Civic Networking ....mfidelman@world.std.com
Cerf, Vinton G..vcerf@CNRI.reston.va.us
CFMT-TV...cfmtv@chicken.planet.org
CFTO-TV..cftotv@chicken.planet.org
Chenevey, Jim..71021.173@compuserve.com
Cheng, William Chia-Wei....................................william@cs.ucla.edu
Chomsky, Noam...chmosky@athena.mit.edu
Christensen, Don ....djc@acuson.com
Christy, Paul ....kpchristy@esa.doc.gov

```
Churbuck, David .......................................................dbuck@well.sf.ca.us
City of Toronto ...............................................toronto@chicken.planet.org
CityTV.............................................................citytv@chicken.planet.org
CJOH-TV...........................................................ab363@freenet.carleton.ca
Clampett, Jed......................................................jedclampet@aol.com
Clancy, Tom........................................................tomclancy@aol.com
Clarinet Information ...............................................info@clarinet.com
Claris ...........................................................................claris@aol.com
Claus, Santa ...........................................................Santa@north.pole.org
Clede, Bill .............................................76702.2011@compuserve.com
Cline, Craig .....................................................110–3939@mcimail.com
Clinton, Bill .............................................President@Whitehouse.gov
Clinton Administration..............................75300.3115@compuserve.com
Cockburn, Craig ................................................craig@scot.demon.co.uk
Cohen, Gregory ...............................................................gcohen@panix.com
Coke Machine .............................................finger drink drink.csh.rit.edu
Cole, Allan .................................................75130.2761@compuserve.com
comp.ai.nlang-know-rep......................................nl-kr-request@cs.rpi.edu
comp.ai.vision .....................................................vision-list-request@ads.com
comp.archives...........................................comp-archives@msen.com
comp.binaries.acorn .............................................moderator@acorn.co.uk
comp.binaries.amiga ...........................................amiga-request@uunet.uu.net
comp.binaries.atari.st.....................atari-binaries@twitterpater.eng.sun.com
comp.binaries.ibm.pc ..........................ibmbin-request@crdgwl.crd.ge.com
comp.binaries.mac................macintosh-request%felix.uucp@uunet.uu.net
comp.binaries.os2.......................os2bin-request@csd4.csd.uwm.edu
comp.bugs.4bsd.ucb-fixes ...............ucb-fixes-request@okeeffe.berkeley.edu
comp.compilers............................compilers-request@iecc.cambridge.ma.us
comp.dcom.telecom ...................................telecom-request@eecs.nwu.edu
comp.doc.......................................................comp-doc@ucsd.edu
comp.doc.techreports.........compdoc-techreports-request@ftp.cse.ucsc.edu
comp.graphics.research .........................graphics-request@scril.scri.fsu.edu
comp.lang.sigplan..............................sigplan-request@bellcore.com
comp.laser-printers ..............................................furuta@cs.umd.edu
comp.mail.maps ................................................uucpmap@rutgers.edu
comp.newprod......................................newprod-request@chg.mcd.mot.com
comp.org.fidonet.......................................................pozar@hop.toad.com
comp.os.research...................................................darrell@cse.ucsc.edu
comp.parallel.............................hypercube-request@hubcap.clemson.edu
comp.patents .................................................................pjt@cs.su.oz.au
comp.protocols.kermit ..........info-kermit-request@watsun.cc.columbia.edu
comp.research.japan ...............................................rick@cs.arizona.edu
comp.risks............................................................risks-request@csl.sri.com
comp.simulation............................simulation-request@uflorida.cis.ufl.edu
comp.society...........................................socicom@auvm.american.edu
comp.society.folklore ............................................eric@snark.thyrsus.com
comp.sources.3b1.........................................dave@galaxia.newport.ri.us
comp.sources.acorn ..............................................moderator@acorn.co.uk
comp.sources.amiga ...........................................amiga-request@uunet.uu.net
comp.sources.apple2 .................................................jac@paul.rutgers.edu
comp.sources.atari.st.....................atari-sources@twitterpater.eng.sun.com
comp.sources.games ..............................games-request@saab.cna.tek.com
comp.sources.hp48........................................spell@seq.uncwil.edu
comp.sources.mac ................macintosh-request%felix.uucp@uunet.uu.net
comp.sources.misc ............................sources-misc-request@uunet.uu.net
comp.sources.reviewed .............................................csr@calvin.doc.ca
comp.sources.sun ...........................................mcgrew@aramis.rutgers.edu
comp.sources.unix...........................unix-sources-moderator@pa.dec.com
comp.sources.x .....................................................x-sources-request@msi.com
comp.std.announce...............................................klensin@infoods.mit.edu
```

If tribbles are as kosher as elephants and rabbits, then they're

comp.std.mumps ....std-mumps-request@plus5.com
comp.std.unix ....std-unix-request@uunet.uu.net
comp.sys.amiga.announce ....zerkle@cs.ucdavis.edu
comp.sys.amiga.reviews ....honp9@menudo.uh.edu
comp.sys.concurrent ....concurrent-request@cortex.neusc.bcm.tmc.edu
comp.sys.ibm.pc.digest ....info-ibmpc-request@simtel20.army.mil
comp.sys.m68k.pc ....info-68k-request@ucbvax.berkeley.edu
comp.sys.mac.announce ....werner@rascal.ics.utexas.edu
comp.sys.mac.digest ....info-mac-request@sumex-aim.stanford.edu
comp.sys.next.announce..................csn-announce-request@media.mit.edu
comp.sys.sun ....sun-spots-request@rice.edu
comp.theory.info-retrieval ....engle@cmsa.berkeley.edu
comp.virus...krvw@cert.sei.cmu.edu
CompuServe ....@compuserve.com
The Computer Page Independent (London Newspaper)...........................
....comppage@independent.co.uk
Computer Professionals for Social Responsibility .....cspr@csli.stanford.edu
Condon, Christopher ....bitlib@yalevm.ycc.yale.edu
Congressional Comment Desk...........................comments@hr.house.gov
Congressional Subcommittee on Telecommunications and Finance ....
....congress@town.hall.org
Conley, Clare ....76057.3613@compuserve.com
Connectix ....connectix@applelink.apple.com
Connors, Dennis ....dconnors@access.digex.net
Coopersmith, Sam ....samaz01@hr.house.gov
Copley, Thomas P. ....go_pher_it@netcom.com
Coronel, Gus..gus@phantom.dot.gov
CoStar ....costar@aol.com
Cotter, Wayne ....73223.1667@compuserve.com
Council, Christopher...meep@mit.edu
Cox, David ....paradox@peg.apc.org
Cristy, John ....cristy@dupont.com
Crummey, Joe............................71075.3111@compuserve.com
Csere, Csaba.............................71234.273@compuserve.com
CTV Television Network ....ctv@chicken.planet.org
Cultural Resources ....cultural@aol.com
Cunningham, Rip ....76424.1525@compuserve.com
Currid, Cheryl ....currid@radiomail.net
Curry, Adam ....acurry@mtv.com, adam@mtv.com
Curry, David A. ....davy@ecn.purdue.edu
Cytowic, Richard E..p00907@psilink.com
DacEasy, Inc. ....daceasy@aol.com
Damme, Aki ....adame@snm.com
David, Peter A. ....pad@cup.portal.com
Davidson & Associates.......................................davidson@aol.com
Davis, Frederic E. ....3057504@mci-mail.com
Dawkins, Freddie ....70624.557@compuserve.com
Dayna Communications.......................................dayna@aol.com
De La Fe, Alfredo..delafe@phantom.com
DeBoer, Dale ....drdeboer.uccs.edu
December, John ....decemj@rpi.edu
Delphi ....@delphi.com
DeMille, Cecil B. ....CecilBdmil@aol.com
Denton, Cynthia................................cynthia@bigsky.dillon.mt.us
Dern, Daniel..ddern@world.std.com
Diamond, David...davidd@uworld.com
Dibbell, Julian..julian@panix.com
Dickey, Jay...jdickey@hr.house.gov
Digital Vision..digital@aol.com
Diller, Barry ....71043.3616@compuserve.com

Direct Software ....direct@aol.com
Dodd, Senator Christopher ....sendodd@dodd.senate.gov
Donovan, Johnny..............................72567.2022@compuserve.com
Dove Computer ....dove@aol.com
Downey, John ....jmd@cyclone.bt.co.uk
Downs, Steve..................................sdowns@oash.ssw.dhhs.gov
Dozier, Jason E. ....71022.220@compuserve.com
Drescher, Patryk.................................drescher@access.digex.net
Drinkard, Michael...................................miked@phantom.com
Dubl-Click Software......................................dublclick@aol.com
Duck, Howard the ....Howardduck@aol.com
Duncan, Ray...duncan @cerf.net
Dvorak, John...................................3184192@mcimail.com
Dyckhoff, Roy ....rd@cs.st-and.ac.uk
Dyson, Esther ....5113763@mcimail.com
EasyNet...@host.enet.dec.com
Ebert, Roger...................................73136.3232@compuserve.com
Ecker, David V...................................decker@ic.sunysb.edu
Effinger, George......................76050.1300@compuserve.com
Electric Image ....electric@aol.com
Electronic Frontier Foundation...................................eff@eff.org
Electronic Mail Association (EMA)..............70007.2377@compuserve.com
Elenay Creations Software...............................elenay@aol.com
Emigre Fonts..emigre@aol.com
Engst, Adam ....72511.306@compuserve.com
Ernst, Dave ....74230.167@compuserve.com
Erwin, Brian...brian@ora.com
Evans, James ....surf93@well.sf.ca.us
Eye Weekly....................................eye@chicken.planet.org
Eytan, Michel ....eytan@suzuka.u-strasbg.fr
Fairbairn, Garry ....76475.606@compuserve.com
Farallon...farallon@aol.com
Farrow, Rik ....rik@uworld.com
Feist, Raymond E......................76657.2776@compuserve.com
Feldman, David...................................feldman@pipeline.com
Ferguson, Alistair..................................utopia@peg.apc.org
Ferguson, George ....ferguson@cs.rochester.edu
Feuerhelm, Jon...jonf@uworld.com
Fifer, Susan Canby ....netgo3@capcon.net
Fifth Generation ....fifth@aol.com
Fisk, Rick ....risk@auspex.com
Fitzsimmons, Ed...................................fitzsimmons@charm.isi.edu
Flack, Dave ....davef@uworld.com
Flansburg, Scott ....76450.3164@compuserve.com
Fleet, Bill....................................72731.360@compuserve.com
Fleming, Art ....artfleming@aol.com
Flower, Joe ....bbear@well.sf.ca.us
Foley, Tod ....asif@well.sf.ca.us
FontBank...fontbank@aol.com
Fox, Jack ....jfox@esusda.gov
Free Software Foundation ....gnu@prep.ai.mit.edu
Frey, Donnalyn......................70277.2502@compuserve.com
Frost, Jim...jimf@centerline.com
Fulghum, Robert......................70771.763@compuserve.com
Fuller, Desmond...................................fuller@hlsun.red-cross.org
Funke, R. W...funke@usc.edu
Gabriel, Gail ....73510.1561@compuserve.com
Garcia, Jerry ....jgarcia@aol.com
Garfinkel, Simson ....simsong@nextworld.com
Garnett, Cheryl ....cgarnett@esusda.gov

Garton, Andrew..agarton@peg.apc.org
Gasperini, Jim...jimg@well.sf.ca.us
Gates, Bill ....billg@microsoft.com
Gateway ....72662.164@compuserve.com
Gateway ....72662.163@compuserve.com
Gateway ....75300.1300@compuserve.com
GCC Technologies ....gcc@aol.com
Gejdenson, Sam...bozrah@hr.house.gov
GeoWorks...geoworks@aol.com
Gerrold, David...70307.544@compuserve.com
Giles, Aaron ....giles@med.cornell.edu
Giles, John ....gilestv@echonyc.com
Gill, Jonathan ....jgill@esusda.gov
Gillin, Paul...76537.2413@compuserve.com
Gillmor, Dan ....dgillmor@det–freepress.com
Gilman, Tim ....tdgilman@ce.berkeley.edu
Gingrich, Newt ....georgia6@hr.house.gov
Gleason, Michael...mgleason@cse.unl.edu
Gleick, James ....gleick@pipeline.com
Global Television Network ....global@chicken.planet.org
Global Village Communication ....global@aol.com
gnu.*...info-gnu-request@prep.ai.mit.edu
Godin, Seth..SGP@sgp.com
Godwin, Mike ....mnemonic#eff.org
Goggans, Chris..erikb@phantom.com
Gore, Al ....vice.president@whitehouse.gov
Graham, Nicholas...joeboxer@jboxer.com
GraphiSoft...graphisoft@aol.com
Green Party of Canada...................................green@chicken.planet.org
Greenbaum, Joshua ....jgreenbaum@mcimail.com
Greenhow, Steve ....73557.1143@compuserve.com
Griggs, Robyn ....rgriggs@panix.com
Grisham, John E. ....71035.1742@compuserve.com
Grodin, Charles ....CharlesGrodin@aol.com
Groening, Matt...mgroening@tv.fox.com
Gronbeck, Christopher ....gronbeck@access.digex.net
Gross, Jay..72517.326@compuserve.com
Grote, Patrick ....71031.335@compuserve.com
Groves, Brent..71760.660@compuserve.com
Grundner, Tom ....aa0011@nptn.org
Guglielmo, Connie...................................connie.g@applelink.apple.com
Gumbleton, Mary Clare ....mcgumble@inet.ed.gov
Gutmann, Peter..pgut1@cs.aukuni.ac.nz
Haahr, Paul..haahr@kaleida.com
Hadingham, Evan ....evan_hadingham@WGBH.org
Haldane, Marilyn.....................................71543.1541@compuserve.com
Hall, Ed ....76117.1245@compuserve.com
Hall, William ....hall.william@epamail.epa.gov
Halpern, Jeremy ....verge@delphi.com
Hargadon, Tom ....foxhedge@well.sf.ca.us
Harris, David...david@pmail.gen.nz
Harris, David ....73057.2663@compuserve.com
Harris, Ellen Key...ekh@panix.com
Harris, Guy ....guy@auspex.com
Harris, Joe...midx@aol.com
Harris, Linda..lharris@oash.ssw.dhhs.gov
Harris, Michael...ontpc@chicken.planet.org
Harris, Paul..73030.2227@compuserve.com
Hart, Michael...hart@umd.cso.uiuc.edu
Hartley, Jim ....jehartley@ucdavis.edu

Haworth, Steven ....sjh@idm.com
Hayden, Patrick Neilsen ....pnh@panix.com
Hazeltine, Andrew..andy@thomas.ge.com
Heintz, Claude...............................76120.1220@commpuserve.com
Helbing, Ralf....................................helbing@engin.umich.edu
Henrichsen, Lonn.............................lhenrich@phantom.dot.gov
Henshaw, Bob ....bhenshaw@hr.house.gov
Herbert, Tom ....therbert@umiami.ir.miami.edu
Hesketh, Richard ....rlh@ukc.ac.uk
Heslop, Brent ....bheslop@shell.portal.com
Heyman, Mat ....heyman@micf.nist.gov
Hires, Ken...............................71303.613@compuserve.com
Hoare, Rob ....72461.3361@compuserve.com
Hoffman, Martin ....100144.447@compuserve.com
Hofstadter, Douglas..........................dughof@cogsci.indiana.edu
Hook, Andy.......................................anselm@web.apc.org
Hoskins, Bob ....75300.1313@compuserve.com
Howe, Walt ....walthowe@delphi.com
Hubbard, Libby ....neutopia@educ.umass.edu
Hughes, Dave ....dave@oldcolo.com
Hunsinger, Ron ....Ron.Hunsinger@bmug.org
Hunter, Ciara...............................73404.3631@compuserve.com
Hutchison, Andrew................................100236.3005@compuserve.com
Idol, Billy..........................idol@well.sf.ca.us, idol@phantom.com
ieee.announce ....burt@ieee.org
Ihnatko, Andy ....andyi@world.std.com
Infocom ....infocom@aol.com
Inline Design ....inline@aol.com
Jeffries, Walter ....73130.1734@compuserve.com
Jillette, Penn ....penn@delphi.com
Jittlov, Mike...........................jittlov@gumby.cs.caltech.edu
Jobs, Steve...sjobs@neXT.com
Johnfelt, Eric..................................ejohnfel@ic.sunysb.edu
Johnson, Brian ....Bjohnson@panix.com
Johnson, Don ....71631.42@compuserve.com
Jones, Michael ....mtj@sgi.com
Joseph, Paul ....72072.146@compuserve.com
Jung, Robert ....robjung@world.std.com
Kadrey, Richard.................................kadrey@well.sf.ca.us
Kahle, Brewster..................................brewster@wais.com
Kapor, Mitch ....mkapor@eff.org
Karten, Naomi ....76217.1620@compuserve.com
Katz, Bruce ....katz@well.sf.ca.us
Kauffman, Bruce.......................72520.1674@compuserve.com
Kawasaki, Guy...........................76703.3031@compuserve.com
Kay, Alan ....Kay2@applelink.apple.com
Kehoe, Brendan ....brendan@cygnus.com
Keillor, Garrison..............................gkeillor@madmax.mpr.org
Kellner, Mark ....kellner@psilink.com
Kemske, Floyd ....73437.50@compuserve.com
Kennedy, Rod ....rod@faceng.anu.edu.au
Kennedy, Shirley Duglin...........................kenneds@firnvx.firn.edu
Kennedy, Ted ....ccasey@hr.house.gov
Kent Marsh ....kentmarsh@aol.com
Keppler, Kay ....72212.3256@compuserve.com
Kerrey, Bob ....tschoeb@hr.house.gov
Kibo..kibo@world.std.com
Kime, J. William..................adm.kime/g-c01@cgsmtp.comdt.uscg.mil
Kimura, Doreen ....kimura@uwovax.uwo.ca
Kingston, Jeffrey H..jeff@cs.su.oz.au

To: Ilene Schneider 72467,3255 (X) The problem was we couldn't get elephants

Markoff, John...Markoff@nyt.com
Martin, John E...............................70304.2276@compuserve.com
Mashey, John...mash@mips.com
Masie, Elliot...............................76703.4375@compuserve.com
Matchette, Lisa ....lisamat@microsoft.com
Mattocks, Craig ....craig@nhc-hp0.nhc.noaa.gov
Maxis ....maxis@aol.com
McBride, Jim..jimm@netmail.com
McCaffery, Simon...................................76216.3013@compuserve.com
McCaffery, Simon...................................76216.3013@compuserve.com
McCaffrey, Anne................................72007.45@compuserve.com
McCarthy, John ....jmc@sail.stanford.edu
McCormack, Chief.............................mccormac@chicken.planet.org
McDonald, Dan.......................dmcdonld|Rv08@rvdc.unisys.com
McGhee, Bonnie ....bonniem@uworld.com
MCIMail ....@mcimail.com
McIntyre, Vonda N. ....72077.61@compuserve.com
McLeod, Lyn...ontlib@chicken.planet.org
McManus, Pat ....72010.511@compuserve.com
McNaught, Judith....................................76416.1065@compuserve.com
MECC...mecc@aol.com
Media Page ....mpage@phantom.com
Meikle, Marg...Marg_Meikle@mindlink.bc.ca
Merenbloom, Paul ....70743.3524@compuserve.com
Meridian Data ....meridian@aol.com
Meseguer, Jose ....meseguer@csl.sri.com
Metcalf, Bob ....bob_metcalf@infoworld.com
Metcalfe, Jane...jane@wired.com
Metro Toronto Zoo..............................mtzoo@chicken.planet.org
Meyer, Claude Erik..cmeyer@nyx.cs.du.edu
Michaels, Art...................................76247.624@compuserve.com
Michelson, Avra ....tmi@cu.nih.gov
Micro Dynamics ....microdynamics@aol.com
Microcom ....microcom@aol.com
MicroMat Computer Systems....................................micromat@aol.com
Micron Technology..micron@aol.com
MicroProse ....microprose@aol.com
Microseeds Publishing..microseeds@aol.com
Microsoft ....microsoft@aol.com
The Middlesex News ....sysop@news.ci.net
Mikes, Steven ....editor@unx.com
Milhoun, Judith ....stjude@phantom.com
Miller, Geoff..geoff@purplehaze.sun.com
Miller, George ....GEORGEM@HR.HOUSE.GOV
Miller, Michael...mikeym@well.sf.ca.us
Milliken ....milliken@aol.com
Mingus, Nancy Blumenstalk.....................71601.2360@compuserve.com
Minister of Agriculture ....agricult@chicken.planet.org
Minister of Consumer and Corporate Affairs...
....consumer@chicken.planet.org
Minister of Fisherie/Oceans ....fisherie@chicken.planet.org
Minister of Health and Welfare ....health@chicken.planet.org
Minister of Labour ....labour@chicken.planet.org
Minister of National Revenue.........................revenue@chicken.planet.org
Minister of Supply and Service........................supply@chicken.planet.org
Minister of the Environment ....environ@chicken.planet.org
Minister of Transportation ....transpor@chicken.planet.org
Minsky, Marvin ....minsky@ai.mit.edu
Mirror Technologies..mirror@aol.com
misc.activism.progressive...................map-request@pencil.cs.missouri.edu

misc.handicap ....wtm@bunker.shel.isc-br.com
misc.news.southasia...................................surekha@isis.cs.du.edu
misc.security ....security-request@rutgers.edu
Mitchell, James...jmitchel@inet.ed.gov
Montulli, Lou ....montulli@ukanaix.cc.ukans.edu
Moolenaar, Bram..mool@oce.nl
Morgan, Robert W. ....72427.723@compuserve.com
The Morino Foundation.....................................mmorino@morino.org
Morning Journal..............................mamjornl@freenet.lorain.oberlin.edu
Morrison, Toni ....morrison@pucc.princeton.edu
Mulroney, Brian..primemin@chicken.planet.org
Murphy, Kevin W.............................71023.3506@compuserve.com
NASA Headline News ....nasanews@space.mit.edu
Nathan, Paco Xander..............................pacoid@well.sf.ca.us
The National Institutes of Health CancerNet...
....cancernet@icicb.nci.nih.gov
National Public Telecomputing Network..........................tmg@nptn.org
National Research & Education Network............nren-discuss@uu.psi.com
NBC News ....nightly@nbc.com
Neal, Joe ....djkiller@aol.com
Negroponte, Nicholas.....................................nicholas@media.mit.com
Nerlich, David ....babel@peg.apc.org
New Democratic Party of Canada...................ndpcan@chicken.planet.org
New Era...newera@aol.com
news.announce.conferences ....denny@tekbspa.tss.com
news.announce.important...............................announce@stargate.com
news.announce.newgroups.......................................tale@rpi.edu
news.announce.newusers ....spaf@purdue.edu
news.answers ....news-answers-request@mit.edu
news.lists ....news-lists-request@cs.purdue.edu
news.lists.ps-maps ....reid@decwrl.dec.com
Niehaus, Ed ....niehaus@well.sf.ca.us
Norcross, Bryan ....PSMw29a@aol.com
Norris, Don ....100032.1151@compuserve.com
Norris, Jon...jon.norris@aquila.com
Norskog, Lance ....thinman@netcom.com
Norstad, John...jln@nwu.edu
Novak, Karen ....knovak@usr.com
Now Magazine...now@chicken.planet.org
Now Software ....now@aol.com
Nuwer, Henry.............................76004.1761@compuserve.com
O'Brien, Larry...............................76702.705@compuserve.com
O'Brien, Miles ....70273.2064@compuserve.com
Object Factory ....objectfactory@aol.com
Office of Technology Assessment...............................elecdelivery@ota.gov
Oikarinen, Jarkko ....jto@rieska.oulu.fi
Ojeda, John....................................11ojeda@gallua.galludet.edu
Oldham, Jim...............................76507.1702@compuserve.com
ON Technology ....on@aol.com
Online Career Center...occ@msen.com
Ontario Human Rights Commission ....onthumrt@chicken.planet.org
OptImage Interactive Services ....optimage@aol.com
Orkin, Richard...............................74250.110@compuserve.com
Ottawa Citizen......................ottawa-citizen@freenet.carleton.ca
Ousterhout, John....................................ouster@sprite.berkeley.edu
Overton, Rick ....72162.1701@compuserve.com
Paige, Ryan ....71172.3532@compuserve.com
Pan, Yi..pan@hype.cps.udayton.edu
Parham, Greg...gparham@esusda.gov
Parisien, Roch ....75010.2074@compuserve.com